I

𝓜

Mosley Publishing Group
P.O. Box 586502
San Diego, CA 92058-6502
www.mosleypublishing.com

Editing by: Lorna Hartman, LetterCraft
Cover by: Bryn Starr Best
Interior by: Stacy Hodge, PD Graphics

ISBN 1-886185-15-8
Library of Congress Control Number: 2002101567
1st printing, January 2002
Printed in The U.S.A.

There Were No Parents Here

 Series One

From The Eyes of a Child

This book is dedicated to God

"The Author and Finisher of My Faith"

Thank you for molding me into the beautiful
woman I am today. I know that I am not everything
I want to be, but I am not what I used to be.

Today I give to you what you have given me,
Love.

A letter from the author . . .

I wrote this book that our nation would listen to its children. What seems un-important to an adult may be devastating to a child. The outcome of every child's life will impact our society for better or for worse.

I live three minutes away from Santana High School in California, the second violent school shooting following on the heels of Columbine in Colorado. When I heard about the shootings on the radio, my heart sank. My book was sched-uled for release in less than two weeks, and I wish now that I had gotten it out earlier so I could share with the world the importance of listening to the silent cry of a child.

I picked up my first weapon at age seven. Like Andy Williams at Santana High, I was a good student with good grades. My classmates made fun of me because I was poor. I bought my first gun at 18 right over the counter in a pawnshop.

This anger and rage are real in our children and teenagers. They will act it out through adulthood if we don't begin to change our parent-child relationships with them.

In my public speaking, I share from the experiences I wrote about in my books so we may better understand the underage assailant, move toward forgiveness, and step out of the "I'm the parent, so do as I say" attitude. The children are aware that we are the parents. We can start by meeting them where they are today. If you as a parent don't like rap music, and your children know this, they'll turn it—and you—off when they see you coming. But if you pretend to like it for only 15 minutes of your day, you will be amazed at what you'll learn about your child. Your child will begin to share with you what he or she is sharing with peers.

I am more than happy to share with you my experience, strength, and hope.

Janice Higgins, author
There Were No Parents Here
Series One ~ From the Eyes of a Child

Response from the author, write to:
Janice Higgins Books
P.O. Box 1947
El Cajon, CA 92022
or e-mail: higgins357@cs.com

CHAPTER 1

 HOW DID I GET HERE?

Here I stand on the second floor, staring out a 12 – inch window. Directly in front of me is a sign reading "NO WARNING SHOTS FIRED."

I can see a guard pacing back and forth in slow motion. A second guard stands at the control panel, yelling "Step in!" as he operates the iron doors. They open and close with a loud clang, iron to iron, metal to metal. One by one, each inmate moves quickly into her cell.

A third guard stands at the end of the tier, pointing and issuing directions. He speaks, but with no expression on his face – like a robot trained to tame wild animals.

I look around for a window. I think to myself, "Maybe there's a way out of here." But there are no open windows. There is no way out.

The lights on the ceiling are large and very bright. They're at different heights, hanging directly into the cells so the guards can easily watch us.

Under the control booth are two pay phones and a sign that read "Three Minutes Only." I read the sign and wonder if they will shoot us for staying on the phone too long.

To my right by the telephones are shower stalls with iron bars. There's a solid square piece of metal in the middle of the bars designed to cover breasts and buttocks while inmates are showering. However, it doesn't do that; I can see the guard on the second floor at the control panel looking into the showers. Next to the showers are six shiny silver tables bolted to the floor.

I look up at the ceiling and say to myself, "Janice, you blew it this time. You finally made it to the big house."

I turn around and look into my cell. Dirty brown brick walls have graffiti written on them. Girls have written messages to their girlfriends or autographed the walls with the last date they were here. Some messages even say they'll be back next year.

To my right are a silver toilet, sink, and water fountain, all connected. I push the button to see if the fountain works. The water drips into the toilet. Do they expect us to drink this water? I'm not drinking this water, I think to myself. I don't think so.

To my left is a set of steel bunk beds and a little desk with writing paper and a pencil stub on it. The mattresses on the beds are very thin and spotted with bloodstains.

The guards give me two thick dark gray wool blankets. They look warm. The sheets are white as snow and smell like the fresh air of springtime.

As I stare out the tiny window of my cell, I ask myself, "How did I get here?" Somehow, somewhere, something in my life went wrong. Prison was not in my plan for my life.

I pace the floor in a dark gray prison – issue muumuu. I try to think about the incident that led to my arrest.

As I'm deep in thought, I hear a voice deep inside speaking sternly to me. It says, "The arrest has nothing to do with why you're here." When I hear this, I feel such a sense of confusion. I continue to pace the floor from the tiny window to the iron bunk beds and back again. Back and forth I pace and think.

I fall on my knees by the bed, crying hysterically to God. I don't really know who He is, but I know His name is Jesus. I ask Him, "How did I get here?" I'm quiet, waiting for an answer, but I hear nothing. I rise from the floor, look around at the brown brick walls, and think to myself, "It will be a long time before I leave here."

What are my children going to do without me? Will they do the same thing I did without my parents? I bow my head and reminisce about my childhood. I ask myself again, "How did I get here?" and become afraid, for deep within me, I've already found the answer to my question: There were no parents here.

DECEMBER 20. 1967

I will always remember driving through downtown Las Vegas in John's baby blue 1958 Cadillac. John was my mother's boyfriend and the stepfather I would like to forget. But though I try to forget John, I'll always remember the car.

It was a big comfortable car with lots of room in the back seat. I liked to sit backward and look out the back window to say good-bye to Howdy Doody. Howdy Doody was the big electric cowboy on the corner of Fremont Street. He'd wave his giant thumb up and down at me as we drove away. Good-bye, Janice.

One morning in the car I decided to lie down and sleep because it was a long ride to Henderson where we were going. The snow outside made it hard for me to stay warm in my little blue jacket. I curled up tight and managed to sleep most of the way, but as we neared home, I was awakened suddenly by the sound of fire trucks and ambulances whizzing past us with sirens blaring. As we approached our apartment complex, we saw police cars and flashing ambulance lights all over the complex.

We pulled into the parking lot, and I was suddenly afraid. I was not used to the noise and lights and had no idea what was going on. As we pulled closer to our apartment, my mother suddenly started screaming. She opened the car door and jumped out. I watched her waving her arms in the air and pulling her hair as she ran toward our porch.

"My baby, my baby!" I heard her scream as she ran. "Oh, my God, my baby!"

My older brother Matthew was lying on the porch. He looked dead. He had been outside in the harsh cold winter weather all night long. John followed my mother, and I watched him try to calm her, but a police officer blocked their way to the porch.

Suddenly a bright light flashed from the sky. It was a medical helicopter hovering directly overhead. A powerful and official – sounding voice shouted for people to make room for a landing. As the helicopter descended, police ordered people to move their cars.

Nobody wanted to leave. Everybody wanted to watch. They wanted to get a peek at my half – dead brother on the porch. They couldn't believe he had been outside all night.

I wanted to get out of the car to be with my brother, but before John had gone after my mother, he'd told me to stay in the car.

I watched from the car window as the paramedics rushed in and started mouth – to – mouth resuscitation. I was in shock, watching everybody running around as they tried to save my brother's life. When they put him on a stretcher and lifted him into the helicopter I was afraid I would never see him again.

Today I know I could have been right about never seeing him again. My mother told me later that he was almost dead when the helicopter lifted off.

I couldn't say a word as people began to leave and my mother and John came back to the car. I looked at John as he tried to comfort my mother as she got into a police car. This terrified me even more because I thought they were taking her to jail and that I would be alone with John.

But my mother had gone to the hospital to be with my brother. I wondered how she could do something so terrible as to leave her son alone outside in the cold all night.

John brought my baby brother James and me into the apartment. Still stunned, I stared out the front living room window at the cars leaving the scene. I looked up into the sky, and as I held myself rigid to keep from shaking, I whispered to God, "Please, please let my brother live."

I began to cry as I walked over to the big white Christmas tree sitting in the corner of the living room. I plugged in the lights, tears streaming down my face, and sat down cross-legged in the soft light. I flicked a branch on the Christmas tree to watch the flakes fall to the ground and watched in wonder as the lights of the color wheel swirled around me. The tree turned red, blue, yellow, and green. I wondered what Christmas would be like without my brother Matthew. My eyelids felt heavy and drooped as I cried myself to sleep.

The phone woke me shortly after I'd fallen asleep. John answered it, and from what I could understand, we had almost lost my brother. I listened intently as John unconsciously repeated what my mother was saying on the other end of the line. Matthew was in critical condition, but the worst was over. He had pulled through open heart surgery and was going to make it. Unfortunately, he would have to stay in the hospital for a while. I knew my brother wouldn't be home for Christmas, and I cried.

Two weeks later, Matthew finally came home from the hospital. I asked if he'd mind if I looked at his scar. He shook his head and didn't seem to mind as I peeled the sticky white bandage off his skin. "Ouch!" he said as I pulled some of the hair off his chest along with the bandage.

My eyes grew big and my mouth fell open as I looked at my poor brother in shock. He had a large ugly scar with black lines across it – stitches from his chest all the way to his stomach. It was about six inches long.

He whispered, "I'm tired. I need to go lie down." I felt so sorry for him as he walked slowly to his bedroom. I followed him into his room to make sure he was OK and to see if he needed any help. As he laid down in his bed, I covered him up with his blanket and thanked God he was alive and finally at home with me. I knew then that God must have heard my prayer.

As I bent down to kiss my brother, my mother yelled at me from the living room. She wanted me to know she was going to the store to get Matthew some juice. "I'll be right back!" she screamed.

"Sure, you'll be right back," I thought. Her "right back" usually meant three days later.

The doorbell rang as I left Matthew's room and I told John I would get it. I saw all of the neighbors standing outside our door, their arms filled with gifts. They had all kinds of toys, presents, and food for Matthew. He was going to have a Christmas after all. I opened the door and 10 people rushed by me and went right to the Christmas tree. They put present after present under the tree. They put food on the table – more than I had ever seen in my life. I was so happy for Matthew. I knew that these people really cared.

They asked to see Matthew, but I quietly explained that he was sleeping. As they started leaving, my mother came back from her errand. As she came up the sidewalk to the door, the visitors started yelling and screaming at her.

"How could you leave your seven year old boy outside all night in the snow?" they demanded, pointing their fingers in her face. My mother tried to come inside but was blocked by a woman who had been Matthew's babysitter. She started to cry and yelled, "How could you do that to Matthew? This is how I feel about you!" She spit into my mother's face.

My mother wiped the spit from her face and tried again to get in the door. She knew she had done wrong. Gambling all night in a Las Vegas casino is never the best thing for a mother to do, especially with nobody looking after her children alone in an apartment miles away. She knew that locking her son out of his home on a freezing night was not the best way to show her neighbors what a good mother she was. She hung her head and kept her eyes to the floor. In a soft, apologetic voice, she asked if they would kindly move aside and let her in.

John, a big man of Puerto Rican descent, heard the commotion and came to the door. Nobody wanted to mess with him. He had big muscular arms, the type of muscle inmates gain from trying to survive in prison – not surprising, considering he had been released from prison two months before he met my mother. I didn't understand all this, but the neighbors did, and they were afraid of him. As he stepped out of the apartment, they began to scatter. He pulled my mother inside and closed the door.

From that day forward, the neighbors made it difficult for us to live there. When John was not around, they would throw rocks at our windows and eggs at my mother. One day they took paint, the kind you use for advertising in shop windows at Christmas, and painted "Child Abuser" on our window. They said my mother was an unfit parent and could no longer live in the complex.

Their actions matched their hostile words, and soon my mother couldn't take it any longer. We packed up and moved to Las Vegas.

⟶ LAS VEGAS ⟵

Two years later, we were still living in the same apartment we'd lived in since we moved from Henderson, Nevada.

I was very happy. I liked my school and made friends with the neighborhood kids. Dawn and Brad were my two best friends. We wouldn't go anywhere without each other. We went to the store, school, and anywhere else we wanted to go, always together.

My mother, now pregnant, would disappear for days at a time, leaving us with whoever she could find to watch us. But sometimes no one would watch us; she would just leave. It was as if she'd forgotten about what she'd done to Matthew just two years earlier.

I remember one day sitting outside with Dawn and Brad making mud pies and dirt pancakes. The sun was setting, and the cold shadows started creeping in. My friends went home, but even though a light drizzle began coming down, I wanted to play a little longer. But not because I like playing in the rain; I just didn't want to go home. I knew I would be all alone in the apartment. After a while I did go home and looked around. I was right. Nobody was there. When I went back outside to search for my brothers, the skies opened and the rain came pouring down.

All alone, I walked back to the apartment, crying all the way. I tried to open the front door, but I couldn't. It was stuck. I pushed harder and harder. Suddenly, the door opened and popped back on my foot, taking off my middle toenail. I looked down and saw blood gushing from my toe. I started screaming and wailing for my mother. I ran back outside, crying, "Mamma, help me!" Nobody answered. I looked up to the sky asking God where my mamma was. Blood was everywhere.

Within minutes my mother showed up out of nowhere, picked me up, and took me to the emergency room. At the hospital, the doctor wrapped my toe in bandages and showed my mother how to wrap it properly. When we got home, I slept in the bed with my mother. She stayed home with me that night. I couldn't believe it, but I thanked God she did.

A few days later, I watched my mother change the bandage on my toe. I said, "Whoa, Mom, that stinks!" My mother laughed, saying, "that's your toe, not mine!" We began laughing together.

Later that day I stared out the window, wishing I could go outside and play with Brad and Dawn. But I quickly got tired of watching and wishing from the window, so I went upstairs to watch television. As I watched cartoons, I heard a knock at the door.

I thought my mother would get it since she was downstairs in the kitchen, but the knocking continued. I went downstairs to answer the door. At the door was a tall, skinny black man, quiet and friendly. He introduced himself as Herbert and said that he was a friend of my mother. Herbert told me that my mother asked him to wait in the house until she came back from the store. I hadn't known my mother had gone out, so I wasn't sure what to think. Though I had never seen Herbert before, I allowed him to come in. My mother had never taught me not to let strangers into the house. He'd said he was her friend, so I let him in.

I went back upstairs to watch my cartoons. It started getting dark outside and my mother still had not come home. I didn't hear Herbert leave, so as it grew darker and darker outside, I began to wonder if he was still in the house. I quietly walked out of my room and peeked over the rail by the stairs to see if he was still there. He was. Each time I checked, he was in the same place, sitting and waiting.

The fourth time I looked down, he caught me looking and pretended to be asleep. A few minutes later I looked again and he was gone. It was late, and I was getting tired, so I went back in my room to go to sleep. I was fed up with waiting for my mother to come home. I didn't even know if she was going to come home. I had entered my room, taken my pajamas out of the dresser drawer, and started to slip out of my pants when I heard the sound of a door creaking.

At that moment, I turned toward the door to see the shadow of a figure hiding behind my bedroom door. It was Herbert . As soon as I saw him, my eyes widened in terror. I tried to scream, but no sound came out. He was huge and fast. He moved toward me quickly and grabbed my arms. I yelled and screamed. Quickly, he put his strong hands over my mouth to keep me from making any noise. He said he wouldn't hurt me if I didn't scream and kept quiet. I nodded my head OK, but when he removed his hand, I began screaming again. He tried to quiet me as he dragged me to my bed and laid me down. He took his hands off my mouth and began to take my underclothes off. He unzipped his pants and lay on top of me. I told him he was heavy and asked if he would get off me. I couldn't breathe. Just then Matthew opened the front door and called my name.

Chapter 1

"Janice!" he yelled. His tone changed when he looked in the room. "Get off my sister or I'm going to call the police!" he shouted, and immediately ran out of the room and called the police.

Herbert jumped up and ran out of the house with his pants still unzipped. My brother asked me if I was all right. I just cried as he held my hand. Matthew told me he would never leave me alone again. His words made me feel better. I believed him.

Matthew and I told my mother about the incident with Herbert, and she could not believe one of her friends would do something like that. She said she never knew Herbert, and I never saw him again.

On that day, I promised myself that nobody would ever touch me in a bad way again.

Three weeks later, I was outside baking mud pies with Dawn and Brad. Everything seemed fine, but something went very wrong. Unexpectedly, Brad threw a mud pie in my eyes, grabbed me from behind, and started humping me as if we were having sex. I told him to quit. He stopped, but then he said, "You know you like it, and when your mother leaves I'm going to come get in your bed and get on top of you."

My head started spinning. All I could think of was the time Herbert had climbed on top of me, and his quiet whisper, "I won't hurt you." I went numb as the anger began to build inside of me. I was so angry I couldn't think straight. It was as if I had stepped outside of my body and someone else had taken over. I had no control over the dark force within.

I had promised myself nobody would ever touch me that way again. I began walking toward my apartment. My steps became swifter as I became overwhelmed with rage. All I could think of were Brad's words: "I'm gonna get on top of you. I'm gonna get on top of you." His voice merged with echoes of Herbert's voice saying, "I won't hurt you. I won't hurt you." The two voices became one. I had to act.

I opened the door of the apartment and walked fiercely into the kitchen, pulled out the kitchen drawer and took out a sharp little cutting knife. I held the knife tightly in my hand as I turned to walk back outside.

The palms of my hands began to sweat when I saw Brad standing a few feet away from me. He was still making mud pies, unaware of how angry I was. When he saw me coming with the knife in my hand, he got scared and started running toward his apartment. I chased him. I could see the terror in his face as he looked back to see how close I was to him. He couldn't get his front door open.

I drew the knife back and plunged it in his back just as he got the door open. I pulled the knife out of his back and walked calmly home, never looking back. I put the bloody knife back in the kitchen drawer where I had found it and sat on the couch. I felt a sense of relief. Nobody was ever going to hurt me again. I finally knew how I could protect myself. For a few minutes more I sat on the couch, not thinking about much of anything except that I wasn't going to let anyone else hurt me.

Feeling thirsty, I tried to get off the couch to get some water, but suddenly found I couldn't move. I didn't know what was happening; it was like I didn't have control over my body anymore. I was unable to move off the couch. My mind was saying "Get off the couch," but my body was not responding.

Abruptly, the door flew open and Brad's mother stood in my doorway, pointing her finger at me and screaming, "Where is your mother?" Her finger still pointing toward my face, she angrily repeated "Where is your damn mother?" She was enraged, and I was terrified. I didn't know what she might do. I slammed the door. As I walked back to the couch, she kept on yelling.

"You stabbed my son! You stabbed my son!" she shouted, then sobbed, "You hurt my baby." In fear I jumped behind the couch, listening to her cry about how I had hurt her baby. I knew I'd done something very wrong.

Seconds later, there was another knock on the door, it was not a normal knock. It was the sound of a stick banging against the door. I looked outside and saw an ambulance driving away, but I couldn't see who was at the door. In minutes I found out who it was when a voice on the other side of the door called, "It's the police, Janice, open the door. We know you're in there."

I was so afraid I began to shake. The voice called again, but softly this time, "Janice, open the door. No one is going to hurt you." I opened the door. A police officer was standing at the door with my mother's friend Linda, who was supposed to have been watching me, yet had neglected to do so. The police officer knelt down to say to me, "You stabbed a little boy three times in the back and he had to go to the hospital." I didn't say anything. I thought I'd stabbed him once.

The officer asked me where the knife was. I pointed toward the kitchen. He went into the kitchen and pulled the bloody knife out of the drawer. Then he came back to me and said, "I'm going to take the knife. I'm not going to take you to jail because you're only seven, but you can't play with knives." And he left.

When my mother came home the next day, Linda told her what I had done to Brad. My mother took me upstairs and searched wildly. I was terrified as I watched her. She found a beige extension cord attached to the television. She snatched it angrily, knocking the television to the floor with the force of her motion. I stood there trembling as she came toward me. She grabbed my arm and told me to lie on the bed. I did exactly as she said. I was on my stomach and she started whipping me with the extension cord. She whipped and whipped until the blood flowed and the skin peeled from my legs and back. With every lash, she cursed me.

When she finished, I could barely move. I was in so much pain for the next few days I could hardly walk. I hated my mother for beating me. I told myself, "When I grow up, I will never whip my children until they bleed."

I missed a week of school as a result of the beating. My mother lied to the principal, saying I had the flu.

I hated my mother that day.

CHAPTER 2

 1970

We had to move after the incident with Brad. Brads' mother never relented. She told my mother that with her gone as much as she was, I would disappear one day. My mother knew Brad's mother would hurt me, so shortly after the threat from Brad's mother, we move to another complex in Las Vegas. There also, was a new baby in the house.

My mother taught me to change my baby sister's diapers and fix her milk bottles. I did so well that my mother would leave me alone with the baby for hours at a time – sometimes days. There were days I would wake up in the morning only to realize I couldn't go to school because I had to watch my two younger siblings.

James was two and a half and Ava was six months old. There was an unspoken rule that the last one up in the morning, whether Matthew or me, had the responsibility of staying home from school to baby-sit. The only way I could go to school was to get up before Matthew and leave while he was asleep. Unfortunately, if Matthew woke up and saw me getting ready for school, he would make me stay home with the children.

One morning, I saw Matthew roll over in his bed as I was going downstairs to leave for school. I went out the back door, making sure to close it quietly, and ran to the bus stop to get on the school bus. I kept looking back in fear that Matthew would show up at the bus stop before the bus came. I paced back and forth, wishing the bus would hurry up and turn the corner. I had a bad feeling that Matthew was going to show up at any minute.

Finally the bus made it to my stop. It seemed to take me forever to walk to the back of the bus and take a seat by the window. When I raised my head to look out the window, I saw Matthew running toward the bus. He had a very angry look on his face. I kept saying to myself, "Drive off, drive off!" As the bus started to pull away, I looked Matthew straight in the face and rolled my eyes. That was the first and last time I had gotten on the bus before Matthew during our era of baby-sitting responsibilities.

The ride to school was a long one. How I wished I could go to school like all the rest of the children. Their lives appeared to be happy. They always talked about what their parents bought them, the kinds of bikes and dolls they had at home. I wished I could go live in their homes.

There were also times when I wished the bus would never stop. I wanted the bus to just keep going – anywhere as long as I didn't have to go back home. But I couldn't leave my baby sister and little brother at home alone. There would be no one to take care of them.

When I got home from school, I was surprised to see my older brother Barry. He was now 16 and had no interest in the family. He was in his own world, which consisted of wild parties, alcohol, and staying out all night, just like my mother.

The apartment security guards were always looking for him. When they found him, they'd say, "We have found our young alcoholic again."

—— **1971** ——

One day John came home early without my mother. He'd been drinking. He told my brothers to go across the street to the playground and play. I asked to go with them. "No!" John said. "I have something I want you to do. Come here and sit on my lap. Come sit here." He said this with his hands moving up and down his legs, trying to convince me to come sit on his lap. He motioned for me to come to him, but I stood there bewildered and motionless. That made him angry.

His eyes became big and red as he reached for me. "Come here, I said!" he yelled. Frightened, I walked slowly toward him.

"I want to teach you something," he said in a slurred, drunken voice and, picking me up and putting me on his lap, he began to force his tongue into my mouth. I bit his tongue. "Ouch! You dumb bitch!" he shouted. His reflex from the bite caused him to throw me on the floor. Suddenly he grabbed me and threw me across his shoulders. I knew right then that I would get a spanking for sure this time, but I didn't care. I knew he wouldn't try putting his tongue in my mouth again.

As he carried me up the stairs, he smelled as if he had slept in a brewery. The stench of alcohol coming from him was so bad I could hardly breathe. When we reached my bedroom, he tossed me on my bed, stood over me, and placed one hand on my stomach to hold me down. With the other hand he pulled off my underwear, brought it to his face, and smelled it, looking up toward the ceiling. I jumped up and ran downstairs and out the door. I went directly across the street to the playground where Matthew was playing.

Matthew asked, "What's wrong?" I said nothing, I just kept looking across the street at the front door to see if John was coming to get me. Sure enough, he stood at the front door and yelled, "Come get this damn baby! Her diaper needs to be changed." I asked Matthew to come with me. He said, "OK. I want something to eat anyway." We walked into the apartment slowly. Finally the alcohol got the best of John, and he passed out on the floor.

The baby crawled around, putting things in her mouth. She wasn't wet, so I knew John had lied. He was just trying to get me to come back to the house.

It was getting late and James was asleep on the couch. Matthew picked him up and put him in bed. I picked up my baby sister from the floor and took her upstairs to my bedroom. I closed the door and pushed the dresser against my bedroom door to ensure that John could not get in.

I tossed and turned all night, hoping my mother would come home, and eventually I fell asleep. My mother did not come home that night.

At daybreak I heard my mother's voice, so I jumped up and moved the dresser from behind the door. I went downstairs to see if John was still unconscious on the floor. When I looked, he was no longer in the house.

I went into the kitchen where my mother was beginning to make coffee. I said, "Mamma, I have to tell you something." She looked at me and asked, "What is it?" I said, "Yesterday, while you were gone, John put his tongue in my mouth and took my panties off of me and put them on his nose to smell them." She looked up with surprise in her eyes and asked, "He did what?"

She grabbed my hand and walked me to the couch in the living room. "Sit there!" she demanded. Without another word, she went to the kitchen. I could hear her on the telephone, calling the doctor's office and making an appointment for an examination for her daughter "who may have a disease."

I didn't know what disease she meant when I overheard her conversation. After she hung up the telephone, she went upstairs to ask Matthew if he would attend to the children while she took me to the doctor's office. "I'll be right back," she said to Matthew. He replied, "Mom, I don't want to watch your kids all week. Please come back today." My mother rubbed his face with her hands and laughed, saying, "I promise, I will come back today."

Matthew and I looked at each other. We did not think her leaving for days at a time was funny.

My mother and I arrived at the doctor's office where a nurse took us to a little room in the back office. My mother and the nurse stepped outside the room to talk. I went to the door to listen to their conversation. I heard my mother say that John had given her some kind of disease sexually and that she wanted to make sure he hadn't given it to me. When she returned, she appeared calm, but curious. The nurse and my mother came back in the room and my mother handed me a bottle.

"I'll need you to tinkle in this bottle," she said. "Why?" I asked. She said it was because the doctor wanted to make sure everything was OK. I told my mother I didn't need to use the restroom, but she wouldn't accept my answer. She became impatient and started demanding that I give her some urine in the cup. Then she said, "If you don't go in this cup, the doctor is going to cut you open like they did your brother Matthew. Remember the cut on his chest?"

I thought back to when Matthew had come home from the hospital, afraid I might get a scar like his. I finally urinated in the cup. My mother looked relieved. As the doctor came in the room, "Janice, tell me what happened yesterday when John came home," the doctor said gently. I told him John had come home drinking and asked me to sit in his lap, that he put his tongue in my mouth and I bit it. I told him how John took me upstairs to my bedroom, took my underwear off, and placed them on his nose to smell them. I told him that when the underwear was on John's nose, I ran out the door. The doctor asked if that was all he had done. I told him yes.

"Is that what you told your mother?" he asked. I said, "Yes." He said, "Are you sure?" I nodded my head, yes.

The doctor and my mother left the room. They stood outside the door and he asked my mother why she thought I might have a sexually transmitted disease. I was only nine years old. I could hear the doctor ask my mother if she believed me when I told her that I didn't have sex with John. My mother said, "I wanted to make sure Janice was telling the truth about what happened."

The doctor came back in the room without my mother. He told me he believed everything I'd told him.

"It is very important to tell me if you've forgotten anything. Did you forget to tell me anything?" the doctor asked. I said, "No." "Did you forget to tell your mother anything?" he persisted. I said, "No, the reason I told her was so that she could protect John."

He asked, "Why would you want her to protect John? You'd want her to protect you, is that correct?" I told him "No, I could protect myself. I didn't want to hurt John as I'd hurt Brad."

"What did you do to Brad?" asked the doctor. I explained how I'd stabbed Brad after a playground incident.

The doctor's face turned red as he said, "But you're only nine years old." I was seven when I stabbed Brad, I told him.

"So this is how you learned to protect yourself? You have your mother to rely on," he reminded me. He couldn't understand. Moreover, I really didn't want to talk anymore. I asked him if I could please go home. "I'm tired," I said. He replied, "Sure, I will be referring your mother to a different doctor, a psychiatrist to get you the help that you need." He thought I was crazy. The doctor spoke to my mother again and we left the doctor's office.

The ride home was very quiet. Mother did not say a word to me, which was quite all right with me. I really did not want her to say anything anyway.

Later that evening things were quiet around the house. My mother paced the floor. I thought to myself that I shouldn't have told her, but I had to. I knew that if I hadn't, I might have hurt John.

That whole night, I worried that my mother might tell John what I had told her. I was so scared that she would. Finally, I fell asleep. I remember tossing and turning throughout the night, but I felt better in the morning. That feeling didn't last long. John had come home early in the morning. He was yelling and screaming about something – what exactly I wasn't sure.

John and my mother went upstairs to their bedroom. The yelling continued, but as hard as I tried, I could not make out the words. Then there was a loud thump on the ceiling above my head. John rushed downstairs and out the front door, leaving it wide open. I could tell by his face that he was very angry.

Then I wondered if my mother had told John about what happened yesterday. I could hear my mother upstairs crying. Matthew, Barry, and I ran upstairs. There she was, sprawled out on the floor. "Help me," she said softly. He had taken an iron pole-rack and hit her with it. In our apartment, as in most low-income housing, the rack was made of heavy, hard iron, and could be deadly if used as a weapon.

I still couldn't help but wonder if she told him about what happened yesterday. Maybe, I thought, this is the result of me opening my big mouth. I watched as Matthew and Barry picked our mother up from the floor. Something was wrong with her leg. She couldn't stand on it. I'd felt so bad for her that I began to cry.

My mother told Barry to call the police, so he went downstairs to call, then came back upstairs to help my mother. Moments later, there was a knock at the door. It was the police. My mother opened the door. As she started to talk to the police, she saw John's car parked across the street. Though a crack in the door, she told the police officer that everything was all right. She was afraid, and I didn't understand the fear that came across her face.

Mamma knew John would go back to prison if she talked to the police. Mamma knew he would come back and get her before the police got him. She knew that if she told the police he had hit her, the next beating would be worse. I couldn't believe it. I just could not believe that she was going to hide what he had done to her.

After John saw the police officer leave, he came in the house, grabbed my mother by her hair, and slammed her into the wall.

"You want to call the police on me? You want to call the police on me, huh?" he said in a rage. "Well, I'll give you something to tell them!" He pulled her out of the house by her hair and dragged her to the car. The engine was still running. John opened the car door with one hand and violently threw my mother in the car with the other hand. She had no shoes on. I fell to the floor crying as I watched. My mother was screaming. "Stop, John! Don't do this! Don't do this in front of my kids," she screamed repeatedly. John was not listening. Neither was anyone else. He just kept going.

The neighbors came out and watched, but nobody did anything to help. They just stood and watched. My mother pleaded with John to stop. Once he had my mother in the car, John came back in the house and said they were going to the store. "We will be right back," he said. In a calm voice he told us, "Lock the door and don't let anybody in the apartment."

The next morning, John woke me up and told me to get ready for school. "I'll stay home and baby-sit the children. You need to be in school," he said. I thought to myself, "Something is going on here. Him stay home?" I didn't believe it. He even asked me if I needed help combing my hair. I told him I could do it.

I asked, "Where is my mamma?" He said, "Your mamma is still at the store, and if anybody asks you where she is, tell them she's at the store."

I thought this was his way of telling me it was none of my business where my mother was. In my heart, I knew she was not coming home, because she always stayed away from home days at a time.

Nevertheless, John being home was very different. I thought, "Well, maybe he's going to try to be a better parent and stay home and watch the children so I can go to school." But then I thought, "Nah, he'll disappear tomorrow." However, I knew I'd better go to school while I had the chance. It was my first day at school in quite a while.

Chapter 3

 **The Fabulous Father**

My life at home took a different turn. It had been weeks now, and my mother had not returned home from the store. Her friends continued to come by the house asking for her. They knew she was hardly ever home, but now they didn't see her at all.

The next door neighbor was my mother's best friend, Barbara. She was an older woman, maybe in her late 50s. Barbara was always there to help feed us and wash our clothes when my mother didn't come home. Now Barbara started coming over to the house every day, as if checking on us. Every time I told her mother was at the store, she didn't say anything, but the sad look on her face showed disbelief. She continued to be there for us.

John started cooking breakfast for us every day before school. He cooked bacon, eggs, and sausage. If we had cereal, he made sure we had toast and orange juice. He would look at our plates and make sure we ate all our food. He allowed me to go with him to the grocery store to pick out things I liked to eat. I never had to do things like this when my mother was there. My house finally felt like a home, except for the fact that my mother still had not come home.

Saturdays were family time. We had a choice of where we wanted to go – to the park, to the movies, roller skating, or ice skating. My brother Barry never wanted to participate. His priorities were still drinking and partying. Security guards still came looking for him because he always violated the 10:00 p.m. curfew in our apartment complex for teenagers under the age of 18.

I had never seen this side of John when my mother was around. He'd turned into the father I had only dreamed of having. He even became particular about the smaller children and their cleanliness. He made sure they didn't play in the dirt and always had clean clothes. He never asked me to stay home and watch the children again. He also never said anything concerning the incident when he was drunk.

One evening, on family night, we were watching movies. Matthew had just come home from the store with milk and cereal for breakfast the next morning. John was in the bathroom. There was a knock at the door. I didn't ask who it was. I just opened the door. When I did, I saw six white men standing in the doorway, all wearing gray or blue suits. One very tall man with blond hair stepped toward me and asked, "Where is your mother?"

"At the store," I answered. The man knelt down and took my hand. He looked into my eyes and said softly, "Mommy has been gone to the store a long time, huh?" I nodded my head up and down, yes. There was a pause, a long silent pause. My hand was still in his, and he just kept staring at me as if he knew where my mother was. As I stood looking at the men, the silence was broken by the men pulling out guns and swiftly running through the house. One man picked up my baby sister and took her outside. Another man picked up my little brother James and took him outside. One man ran upstairs. Three other men stood by the bathroom door with their guns pointed at John. One man pulled out a badge and yelled at John, "Freeze! FBI! You're under arrest for the murder of Alice Higgins."

Two agents grabbed his hands and placed them behind his back. As they were putting the handcuffs on him, one agent said, "Ms.

Higgins was found right outside of Reno. That gave you plenty of time to kill her and come back here. She was shot five times, and her leg was broken. Oh, but I don't have to tell you that, because you know that. You broke her leg before you killed her." Then he shook his head and said, "I can't believe you would come back here and live as if you've done nothing wrong."

After hearing all of this, I became angry and ran toward the bathroom door, screaming, "Why? Why? Why would you take our mother away from us?" One of the agents held me.

As the FBI agents walked John out of the bathroom into the hallway, I fell to my knees, asking why repeatedly while tears rolled down my face. I wrapped my arms around John's pant leg as the FBI agents were trying to take him away. I pleaded and begged them to let him answer me. Then they suddenly stopped. Nobody moved. They were going to allow him to answer me. But he said nothing. My heart sank to my lap as I slowly let go of his leg, crying hysterically now. One of the agents and Barbara came and picked me up off the floor. We walked outside and sat on the stairs.

The FBI agents walked through the apartment, searching every room. I saw them take things out of John's room and put them in plastic bags. One agent yelled from upstairs, "I found it!"

I watched as they brought the gun outside in a clear plastic bag marked "EVIDENCE." The gun was chrome-colored and big. I thought to myself, He could have killed us all with that big gun. I could not believe I had started to think of him as a perfect father.

We sat outside on the stairs. I looked up to the sky. All my dreams and hopes of my mother coming home had vanished. Barbara asked me if I understood what was going on here. I told her I did. I said, "John pretended to like us, when he really hated us." Barbara asked if I realized we would never see our mother again. I said, " I know what dead means." As I turned my head around, looking for my baby sister and brother, Barbara said, "They're with the FBI agents. We can go check on them if you would like."

I asked her why the men in suits did not have police clothes on. She said that they were special police assigned to find my mother, and that she was sorry it turned out this way.

"Who is going to take care of us?" I asked. She said, "I would like to, but I'm too old." She then asked when my birthday was. I told her March 23. She said, "Well, isn't that special. That's my birthday too." I didn't believe her. I thought she was just trying to make me feel better because I was crying. But I believed her when she went inside her apartment and brought out her birth certificate. She said, "See, I would never lie to you to make you feel better, especially at a time like this. Nevertheless, I want you to know something. I want you to know that from the last day your mother left the house with John, I did all I could to help the police find her. I'm sorry it took so long."

Thinking back, I realized Barbara was probably the reason they found my mother and caught John. She may have saved our lives.

Barbara then held my hand and, squeezing it tightly, said, "I pray that God sends the right people to care for you." I looked at her and smiled, saying, "I know that God will. He always has taken care of me when no one else would." Deep in my heart, I truly believed God would take care of me.

A few minutes later, the agent walked over to me and asked, "Where is Barry?" I told him, "I don't know. Barry always misses curfew." The agent told another agent to call the Las Vegas police to try to locate Barry and take him to a place called Child Havens Receiving Home for Children.

CHILD HAVENS CHILDREN'S CENTER

It was dark by the time the agents finished searching the apartment. The last agent out of the house asked if all the children were in the car. He looked at me and asked if I was ready to go. I told him yes and hugged and kissed Barbara good-bye.

They put all of us in a big white car and drove away. They said they were taking us to a place called Child Havens. It was a long ride. In the car, I wondered what was in store for us and who God was going to send to take care of us.

The car finally stopped and the agents helped us out. We walked up to a big brown building with lots of lights. The agent rang the doorbell and a little tiny woman opened the door. I will always remember her. She was so pretty, with a warm, inviting smile. "Come in, children, my name is Maria," she said softly. "Let me prepare you for bed so that you can get a good night's sleep and we'll talk in the morning." She asked the agents if they could wait until she tucked us in bed, and then she would do the paperwork.

James and Ava went to the room for infants and toddlers. I went to a dorm filled with girls my own age, and Matthew went to a dorm for boys his age. We were in different rooms, but we were all in the same building. I knew I would see my sister and brothers in the morning. They gave me Mickey Mouse pajamas that smelled fresh and clean. I liked that.

The dorm was full of bunk beds. Near the entrance, there was a bathroom with Daffy Duck decorations. I pulled the blankets back on the bed and crawled in. As I lay there, I thought about all that had happened that day. I thought about Barry and hoped they would find him soon. Somewhere, lost in those thoughts, I fell asleep.

The next morning, I could hear the rest of the children in the dorm getting ready for breakfast. I heard the kids saying a new girl was here. I rose and sat on my bed so I could see their faces. There were many children here without parents. A woman came and gave me a toothbrush, towel, comb, and clothes. I rushed to brush my teeth and wash my face. I couldn't wait to see the rest of the children.

I went to the dining room and saw my sister, dressed in pink with a pretty pink bow in her long hair. My brother James had on blue jeans and a blue shirt. They looked so happy. My sister was sitting in a high chair playing with the food she didn't eat. She had never been in a high chair. When she saw me, she reached out her arms. She was very happy to see me. I started feeding her and playing with her at the same time. We had a lot of fun. At that moment, I thought to myself, "This little baby will never know her mother. I'm her mother now and always have been." I paused and looked at how pretty and happy she was. It was as if she didn't have a care in the world.

I pulled James's chair closer to me so I could feed him too. He liked me to play patty-cake with him. He would throw his food on the floor, and I would pick it up. Then he would throw it again. We were having a blast.

Until three black kids walked right up to me and asked me, "Why are you feeding those white kids?" I told them they were my brother and sister.

They called me a liar. "They're white and you're black," they said. "Liar, liar, pants on fire," they laughed.

I began to take my brother and sister out of the chairs and clean them up. The children continued to laugh and make fun of me. One of our caregivers heard them and told them to stop. They stopped for a short time, but continued during dinner.

THREE DAYS LATER

A few days later the FBI agents brought our clothes from the apartment. They laid them out in the middle of the floor and asked us to pick out clothes for the funeral.

They told Matthew and I that we would not be able to see my mother's body. The casket would not be opened because her body had been in the desert too long. We had started picking through the clothes when Maria walked past and asked what we were doing. I told her we were picking out clothes to wear to the funeral.

She gazed at the clothes with a look of disgust.

"No. I will find something pretty for you to wear to the funeral," she said.

"Will you find something for my brothers and sister too?" I asked. "Certainly I will," she said. "I'll take these clothes and throw them away. I will get you some better clothes." Maria picked the clothes up off the floor and placed them in a bag. As she worked, the agent said he would be back on Tuesday to take the children to the funeral. Maria told him she would be going too.

As Maria continued to bag the clothes, I saw a green skirt my mother used to wear. When Maria had turned her back for a moment I reached down, picked up the skirt, and hid it under a table. I didn't want her to throw it away, so I asked Maria if I could keep the skirt. She said no, but told me that if I found something small in the chest, I could have it. I ran to my bed, took the pillowcase off the pillow, ran back to the chest, and started putting silver dollars into the pillowcase. By the time I was done, it was too heavy to lift into my dresser. So I had to drag the pillowcase across the dorm floor after putting some of them in the drawer.

There were many coins. I was rich, and I knew it. This was a secret between God and me. I knew He would take care of me.

THE DAY OF THE FUNERAL

I didn't sleep much last night. In my mind, I revisited the day the FBI came to the house, and I couldn't stop wondering if my mother told John about the incident when he was drunk. Maybe that's why he killed her, I thought. I wonder if telling was the right thing to do. Well, maybe I'll never know.

I sat up in my bed, looked around, and noticed that I was the only one awake. I wondered if it was time to get up and get dressed for the funeral. I walked over to the glass doors of the dorm so I could look out and see the clock on the wall. The clock says 5:00 a.m.

Wow, I thought, I am up pretty early – the funeral isn't until 10:00. I walked back over to my bed and looked at the blue dress, lacy white socks, and shiny back shoes with big bows. I asked myself, "Why do people get dressed pretty to go to a funeral? I'm never going to see my mother again anyway. Besides, she won't see how pretty I am." Suddenly I began to realize, "I must go to the dorm office and tell the caregiver that I don't want to go the funeral."

Immediately, I jumped out of bed and ran toward the office. I saw Susan sitting at her desk. When she saw me, she jumped as if I had frightened her. I said, "I'm sorry if I scared you." "It's OK dear, what's wrong?" she replied.

"Today we're going to my mother's funeral, and I don't want to go. Do I have to go?" I asked. Not able to understand my question, Susan asked, " Why don't you want to go?" She continued with, "Janice, the funeral is for you to say good-bye to your mother for the last time. Besides, all of her friends and your family will be there." When I heard that explanation, I said, "Well, OK. But why aren't my baby sister and brother going?"

"They are too little to say good-bye. You should say good-bye for them. When you get back, you should tell them all about it," she explained. I said, "OK."

On my way back to the dorm, I saw Barry! I could not believe my eyes. I called his name and he turned to see who was calling him.

"I'm going to the restroom. Wait for me," he said. When he returned, I asked him when the police had found him. The previous night, he told me; he had been with his friends, drinking, for the past few days. I told him that the funeral would be today and that the casket would be closed because her body had been in the desert too long. I also told him what time we were leaving. He didn't say much, only asked where the rest of the children were. I showed him where their rooms were. He went back to the dorm for teenagers and I went back to bed.

I was awakened by a soft tap on my leg. It was Maria. "You missed breakfast, but if you hurry and get dressed, I will find you something to eat," she said. I jumped out of bed, took my clothes off the dresser, and went to the restroom. After I finished getting dressed, I walked to the dining area. Maria had a bowl of cereal on the table. While I ate, Matthew and Barry came over to my table. They sure looked different. I had never seen them look so nice. We all stared at each other. I think we were all hoping the caregivers would allow us to keep the clothes.

"Hurry up, Janice!" Maria yelled from the office. Matthew and Barry waited as I put my bowl in the kitchen sink. We walked over to the office. Maria came out and asked us if we were ready to go. We told her we were.

The doorbell rang. It was one of the FBI agents; as we walked out the door with him, I noticed a station wagon parked in front of the building. The agent said we'd be riding in it. But I was looking for that big white car he drove us in when he first brought us here.

I sat in the back seat. It was a long and silent ride. No one said a word. I watched the cars and everything else we passed. I was able to see lots of things as we drove through downtown Las Vegas. There was Howdy Doody again. I hadn't seen him in a long time. He still looked friendly, waving his thumb at me.

I remember thinking that all these people were having so much fun, but I had to go to a funeral. I started clicking the heels of my shoes together. Now, I thought, I'm ready to go and get it over with. I got angry, but I was too afraid to tell anyone how I was feeling.

The car slowed and we turned in next to a gray building. The agent parked the car and everyone got out, then we walked to the front of the building.

There was a short set of steps leading up to two big glass doors. The agent opened the door, and we entered. There were flowers everywhere. People I had never seen before in my life were there crying.

I pulled on Maria's arm. She knelt down.

"Where do people go after they die?" I asked. "To heaven," she said. She took my hand and we walked to the front of the chairs. We sat directly in front of the big gold casket. There were so many flowers. People walked by the casket and said good-bye. I wondered if my mother heard them. Then it was time for us to walk past the casket. I placed my hand on the casket and said "Good-bye, mamma," but somehow it didn't feel like good-bye. I didn't feel like I was going to miss her. I didn't know what I was supposed to feel, but I remember wishing I could have seen her one last time.

I watched Matthew and Barry walked past the same as I had. Unlike everyone else, we didn't cry. We simply watched everyone.

The funeral finally ended and I was ready to leave. The ride back was not as long as the ride going to the funeral. Still, no one said a word. When we pulled up to Child Haven, Maria thanked the agent for taking us. When she opened the door, I ran to the dorm to change clothes, because Maria had said that when we came back from the funeral, I could start school.

I came back to the office almost out of breath. "Maria, Maria, can I go to school today?" I asked anxiously. "Yes," she said. She took me to a room across from the office. It looked like a classroom. I saw drawings of animals. At the top of the chalkboard were the letters of the alphabet. Ms. Barryson walked in the room and introduced herself. She told me that she would be my teacher while I lived in Child Haven Center. She said that normally school starts at 8:00 a.m., and I came right into the classroom. I asked where the rest of the children were. She told me they were outside playing.

There was a hamster named Sammy in the classroom. He was brown with a white stripe down the middle of his chest. I played with him for a while. I had never seen a hamster before. Then the children returned from recess and Ms. Barryson said I could start school tomorrow.

~ **THE NEXT MORNING** ~

The next morning I was up early, eagerly waiting to dress and go to breakfast. I almost choked from eating so fast. Susan, the caregiver, told me to slow down. She also asked me if I had somewhere I needed to be soon. "Yes," I said, "I have to go to school at 8:00 a.m.," I said. She laughed because she knew that the school was in the same building we lived in.

This was my first day and I was excited about being there. I knew all the children from living together. It was not the same as Vegas Verde, the school I'd gone to before my mother died. Here we had one teacher in each classroom. I liked Ms. Barryson, she was nice. We worked from our math and reading books. Then it was time to go outside for recess.

Behind the building were swings, slides, skates, balls, and bikes. I had never ridden a bike before. The first few times I got on the bike I fell off. And just when I began to get the hang of it, recess was over. I was bummed. I wanted to continue learning how to ride that bike. I was so close to keeping it steady. "Recess is over Janice, come on in," Ms. Barryson called.

We returned to the classroom. It was picture painting time. I was to draw and paint a picture of my favorite animal. The only problem was that I didn't have a favorite animal. I never had time to think about animals. My thoughts were always on taking care of my baby sister and brother. I wasn't sure how to tell Ms. Barryson I had never seen an animal. I'd spent most of my time at home watching cartoons on television while baby-sitting my siblings. Ms. Barryson walked around the classroom to see what everyone was drawing. Just as she made her way down my aisle Susan, the caregiver, came to the door. She and Ms. Barryson went to the back of the room to talk.

I heard the doorbell ring as they were talking and asked if I could see if it was Maria. "You sure can, Janice, just don't open the door," Susan said. I ran out to the front door and saw a tall skinny black woman with a funny-looking wig on her head. I ran back to the classroom to tell Susan. "It's not Maria, it's a black lady," I stated. Susan went to answer the door. Shortly afterwards she came back to the classroom and asked Ms. Barryson if she could speak to me. She told me to get my books. I went with Susan to a small room in the back of the office. When we entered the room, the black woman I had seen at the door was sitting there. Susan introduced her as my mother's sister and told me she was here to take us home to Arizona with her.

I didn't know what to say. This was so unexpected. Susan said, "I will leave you two alone so you can talk to your Aunt Gina." I grabbed Susan's hand and pulled her down to me to whisper in her ear. Quietly I said, "Please don't go."

Susan looked at Gina and asked if she would like some water. Gina replied, "Please," with a smile on her face. Susan left to get the water and I continued to stare at this woman and the funny-looking wig on her head. She was wearing a brown dress and brown shoes. There was a silence between us. Susan walked back in the room with the water.

"So, what do you think about going to live in Arizona?" asked Susan. I still didn't know what to say.
"Janice, it's OK. You're probably uncomfortable right now. Take your time and you can say whatever is on your mind," Gina said in a calm, convincing voice. We sat still. No one said anything for about three long minutes. Then the telephone rang and Susan left to answer it.

"I took care of you when you were a little girl," Gina said softly.

Still looking at her, I asked her where my mother had been when she had taken care of me. She told me my mother was a very busy woman. I asked her why I had to go live with her – I didn't know her. I wanted to stay here at Child Haven. She told me this was only a place to live until someone in our family came to pick us up. That told me I didn't have a choice. I was going to Arizona.

I asked if she would be taking all of us. She said, "Well, Ava's father wants to keep her."

I looked at her with surprise and asked, "Who, John?" Gina looked at me with great surprise and said, "John is not Ava's father. Her father's name was Moses."

I was confused, because I had never seen my mother with another man. I was sure Gina had made a mistake. She went on to say that Moses had contacted her asking for Ava. She'd told him that she didn't want us separated, and she would take care of all of us.

I asked her if she had seen my sister and brothers, and she asked me to go get them.

Susan told Matthew and Barry where to go, and we went to the infant dorm to get James and Ava. They were so happy to see me.

Matthew and Barry were in a comfortable conversation with Gina when we had returned. So comfortable that I heard Barry call her Aunt Gina, because he remembered her. She asked to hold Ava. I handed Ava to her.

She took James by the hand. Barry asked, "When are we leaving for Phoenix?" She said it would be next week. She also told us her husband, Danny, would be coming back with her to pick us up.

I asked her, "How will we get to Phoenix?" "By Greyhound Bus," she told me. She asked for a hug and then left.

I wasn't sure I wanted to go, but I had no other choice. I continued to wonder about Ava's real father. I couldn't believe this. It really bothered me. It bothered me so much that I spoke to Maria about it, but she didn't have the answer either.

I went on wondering who James's father was and asked Maria why my brother and sister had the same last name as I did. She told me that my mother had been married when she had me and that she'd given the two little ones her married name after they were born. It was so confusing. I didn't want to talk about it anymore, because I didn't understand. It was almost dinnertime, and I went looking for Barry to ask him if he really wanted to go to Phoenix.

I saw him walking into a room. There was a sign on the door reading "TEENAGERS ONLY." I wondered what was so special about teenagers. I knocked at the door and asked if someone could call my brother Barry.

"Hey Barry, a little kid is at the door to see you," said a boy in a red shirt. When Barry asked who it was, the boy told him it was his sister. I waited about ten minutes before the boy came to the door again and said Barry didn't want to be bothered. I walked away sad, my feelings hurt.

Next I went to the kitchen to see if they needed help washing the dishes. I saw Maria, and instantly the frown I had on my face turned into a smile. I explained to her about Aunt Gina coming to see us, and that we would be leaving with her in a week. She told me she had spoken with my aunt several times on the telephone. She also told me my aunt called several times through the week to ensure we were OK.

Hearing Maria say this made me feel better, and when she told me that my aunt would take good care of us, I wanted to go to Arizona.

CHAPTER 4

PHOENIX, ARIZONA

Over the past week I'd learned to ride a bike, jump rope, and play hopscotch. Although I was not ready to leave Child Haven, I did look forward to going to Phoenix, especially riding the Greyhound bus. All my things were packed, including my silver dollars.

I went to the toddlers' dorm. James and Ava were playing, and their clothes laid neatly on the dresser. I washed James's face and hands and dressed him. Ava was a little harder to dress because she liked to move a lot. I finished getting her dressed and told Susan we were ready.

We brought all our luggage to the front office. I sat in the day room waiting for my aunt to come. The other children came out to say good-bye to us.

The doorbell rang. I ran to look out the window and saw my aunt, but she didn't look the same. She didn't have that ugly wig on her head. She was much prettier without it.

I ran and got Maria. As she went to the door, I followed close behind. As soon as she opened the door I ran to Aunt Gina and hugged her. I was happy because she'd said she would come back – and she did.

"Wow, you sure are ready to go," Gina said in a joyful voice. "I've been waiting for you to take us on the Greyhound Bus," I said happily.

Maria asked her to have a seat while she went to the kitchen to see if our lunches were ready. When Maria came back, Barry helped Aunt Gina put our suitcases in the yellow cab. We were finally leaving. I ran to the classroom to say good-bye to Sammy the hamster. He looked at me with a sad face. I told him he was the first animal I had ever played with in my life and that I would always remember him. Then I kissed him on his head and said good-bye. Everyone got in the cab except me. I just stood there looking at Maria. She took me by my hand and said I was a brave little girl.

"You had to do many things to survive in the few years you have been on this earth. I will always remember you, Janice. I want you to know that what happened in your life with your mother is not your fault," she said. "I love you."

I cried and told her, "No one has ever told me that." She continued, "Most of all, Jesus loves you more." I answered, "I'll always remember you too."

I wiped the tears from my eyes. Maria was crying too as she walked me to the cab. I sat near the window and watched Maria as the car pulled away. She stood there until we drove out of sight. I knew in my heart that she loved me.

From the back seat, Aunt Gina's husband Danny, sitting in the front seat, looked like a huge man. His voice was very deep. He didn't say much to us. The ride to the bus station was not long at all. We drove back through downtown Las Vegas. The cab pulled up to the curb, and the cab driver started taking our luggage out of the trunk of the cab and setting it on the sidewalk. My uncle paid the driver and we walked into the bus station. We sat down as Gina and Danny went to the window to pay for the tickets. Barry and Matthew were very quiet, and I didn't know what to say. I held Ava in my lap as she cried for her bottle. I kept wondering what Phoenix was like. My aunt said it was very hot.

I heard a voice over the intercom say "Boarding to Phoenix." My aunt said, "That's us, you guys, let's go." She took Ava from my lap, and Danny held James by the hand.

Many people were boarding the bus. We decided to sit close to the restroom. The driver announced our arrival time. I counted on my fingers and realized it would take us almost 10 hours to get there. I thought to myself, "*Wow*, that is a long ride." My aunt told us to tell her when we were hungry so she could take out the sack lunches Maria had prepared for us. I watched my aunt play with Ava's hair. She couldn't believe how long Ava's hair was. My aunt played patty-cake and tickled Ava, until Ava fell asleep.

After sleeping awhile, I woke when the bus driver made a sharp turn. I looked out of the window. Mountains looked like big shadows of people moving. I was afraid when I saw them, so I woke Matthew up, trying to tell him about how the mountains looked like people. But since everyone else on the bus was asleep, I decided I needed to go to sleep also.

THE NEXT MORNING

It was early in the morning when we arrived in Phoenix. The bus driver announced our arrival, and everyone woke up and started getting their things off the bus. Our cab was parked outside the bus station. We put our luggage in the cab and were off to my aunt's house.

The cab driver parked the cab two blocks away from where my aunt and uncle lived. "You're going to have to get out here," he said. "I don't want to get robbed, so I'm not going into the Sixteenth Street projects," he explained.

We took our things out of the car and began to walk down the street. The project buildings were two stories of dull dark gray. One street was barricaded with cement from one block to the other to prevent cars from driving in and out of the projects.

In between the long cement blocks were basketball courts and many lights. To my right outside of the building was a recreation center. The name of the downstairs part of the center was the Sidney P. Osborne Projects. As we walked past this building, my aunt told us that was where she worked.

It was a long way to her apartment. We finally made it to her building, which was across from the Sidney P. Osborne Daycare Center.

As we walked up to the door, I could hear the children. "Mamma's home with those kids," they yelled. It sounded like there were a lot of kids inside. When the door opened, sure enough, there were a lot of kids. I remember thinking to myself, "I hope all those kids don't live here," but they did. My aunt and uncle had six kids, plus us, to take care of. This made 11 children in one apartment. I could not believe it.

There were only three bedrooms in this apartment. As I walked in, I looked around. The couch was beige, but so dirty that the beige had changed to brown. My aunt's kids just stood there looking at us as if they didn't want us there. Little did they know the feelings were mutual. They didn't tell us their names. Instead, they whispered among themselves.

I turned and looked at my aunt. "Where are we going to sleep?" I asked. She told me to follow her and we went down the hall. On my right side was a restroom with a sink, a toilet, and a dirty bathtub. Right next to it was another bathroom. This bathroom didn't have a door. It didn't have a bathtub, only a toilet and sink. I saw crayon markings all over the hallway walls.

"Janice, we don't have much. The girls can sleep in one room and the boys in the other, except for you, Barry. Since you are older, you can sleep on the couch," she explained.

In the girls' room were two twin beds and a dresser. I placed my suitcase on top of a bed. One of her kids said, "That's our bed." So I put my suitcase on the other bed. Another of my aunt's daughters said, "That's my bed." So I just set my luggage on the floor.

My aunt told her children to behave and that they must share. She assigned everyone sleeping locations. Under their breath, her kids began to mumble about the sleeping arrangements. It was very clear we were not welcome.

I tried to put the suitcase under the bed, but it wouldn't fit, so I bent down to see why it wouldn't fit. Under the bed were dirty clothes, shoes, and a lot of trash. I left the suitcase on the floor and went to the kitchen to get the broom.

My aunt had taken my baby sister to her room. Meanwhile, the other children stood and watched to see what I was going to do. I saw the broom in the kitchen, leaning on the refrigerator. It only had a few straws left in it, so it was really just a piece of a broom.

The kids stood in the hallway, looking at the broom and laughing, as I walked toward the bedroom. I went in and swept under the bed. After I'd finished sweeping, I picked up the dirty clothes and socks and asked the children where they put their dirty clothes.

Robin, who was my age, said, "I'll show you. Follow me." We went through the kitchen into the pantry, which had a washer and more dirty clothes. I left my stack and returned to the bedroom to finish cleaning. Soon I guessed my aunt's kids had gotten tired of making fun of me, because they decided to go outside to play.

After I finished cleaning the bedroom, it was spotless. When my aunt's kids returned to the house to see if I was finished, a look of surprise was all over their faces. This was obviously an indication that they didn't clean very often.

When I finished cleaning the room, I went to the pantry and sorted the dirty clothes. I separated the dark clothes from the white clothes and pulled the washing machine out of the pantry. I was going to wash the clothes for my aunt. I looked for the dryer, but there wasn't one, so I went to my aunt's room and asked where the clothes' dryer was. She led me through the kitchen and out the back door where she showed me a clothesline. We walked back into the pantry, where she looked for the clothes pins I would need to pin the clothes on the clothesline. "Boy," I thought to myself, "how long has it been since anyone washed clothes?"

After my aunt found the clothes pins, she asked me if I knew how to use the washing machine. I told her I could cook, clean, baby-sit, and anything else she needed. She wanted to know if my mother had taught me how to take care of the house. I told her I had taught myself because my mother was hardly ever home. I had to wash about 11 loads of clothes that day. It was hot in Phoenix, so the clothes dried quickly on the line.

When evening came, I was so tired. First I went to the bedroom to put clean sheets on the bed. After changing the sheets, I sat down to rest and fell asleep. I didn't wake up until the next morning. I got up and looked around. Two of my aunt's children were in bed and two were sleeping on the floor.

I heard someone in the kitchen, so I went to see who it was. It was my aunt, making coffee. She thanked me for washing the clothes and for doing a good job. I told her I was used to cleaning and taking care of things around the house. She said she was on her way to work and that Barry would be watching us.

A look of surprise came over my face. My aunt asked, "What's wrong?"

"That's OK, I'll watch my brother and sister. Barry could watch the rest of your kids," I replied. She questioned, "Why would you say something like that?"

I told her, "Barry has never baby-sat anyone." I knew he was not going to watch over us. She went to his room to ask him to baby-sit, but to her surprise he had not come home all night. I was not surprised at all.

She told me where the cereal was and gave me a dollar to go to the corner store for milk. As she walked out the door to go to work, she told me she would call me on her lunch break.

I looked at the cereal. It was a huge bag of puffed wheat, the kind you have to add sugar to.

My aunt's children came into the living room to watch television. I asked if someone would show me where the corner store was. I needed to buy some milk for the cereal. Alicia told me there was no sugar. I went to my suitcase and counted out five silver dollars, and Alicia and I walked to the store. We bought milk and Froot Loops, the kind of cereal you don't have to add sugar to. We also bought cupcakes, chips, and lots of candy. Alicia was very happy. She didn't want me to tell the other kids we had bought all that stuff; she wanted to be selfish and keep it to herself. I told her no, we were going to share, and if it wasn't enough for everybody, we could always go back to the store. I told her I had more silver dollars at home.

I went to the store all day buying candy for all of us and for other kids in the projects. When my aunt came home, we were all sick. She desperately wanted to know what had happened, so I told her about the silver dollars. She took all my silver dollars and told me she would give them back later. She never did. I was very angry.

⟋⟋ SEPTEMBER OF 1971 ⟋⟋

During the summer things were much the same, but it was more difficult for me because there were more kids in the house. Although my Aunt Gina was home most of the time, she really wasn't.

The 11 loads of clothes had become a daily chore along with cooking duty. My aunt never made her kids do any cleaning around the house. Soon enough the summer ended. School would start tomorrow, and my aunt told me I would be in charge of taking care of the three little kids – my sister Ava, 1; my brother James, 3; and my aunt's daughter Brenda, 2.

I was to get them up in the morning and make sure they were dressed and their hair was combed, then take them across the street to the daycare center. I was to pick them up when I returned from school. This made me angry. Not only did I have to take care of my sister and brother, now I also had to take care of my aunt's youngest daughter.

The first morning was hard. Brenda didn't have much hair, and it was nappy and difficult to comb. I finished dressing the three kids and then dressed myself. I walked everyone over to the daycare center. The people there showed me how to sign the kids in and out when I dropped them off or picked them up.

Mrs. Tavleredis, my fourth grade schoolteacher, looked at me and asked me why I was late to class. I didn't say anything. She asked again, but still I just looked at her. She started walking toward me, and I noticed she had a limp when she walked. By the time she reached my desk, I was standing up.

"What is your name?" she asked. I told her my name, and she told me there would be not recess for me. In a rude tone I told her, "I don't care." She continued with class.

At recess time all the children stood to go outside to play. I Pearl out of my seat and started walking toward the door. "And where do you think you are going?" Mrs. Tavleredis asked. "I'm not staying in here with you," I replied. My teacher walked quickly in the direction of the door, where I was standing. She reached for my arm, but I pulled away. She tried to grab me again. I jerked away, and as I pulled my arm away I knocked over all the books on her desk.

"Look what you have done!" she screamed. "Now, pick them up!" I told her if she wanted them off the floor, she needed to pick them up her damn self. She was very angry and called the principal's office. She told me to go to the principal's office.

When I entered his office the secretary told me to sit down. The principal would be right with me. This black man walked into the office. His legs were bowed and he was short. He looked at me and told me to step into his office. He sat at his desk and told me to sit down.

"What's the problem?" he asked. I told him, "I really did not feel like talking anymore." "I can understand that, but you can't disrupt Mrs. Tavleredis's class. I want you to go back to class and I don't want any more problems out of you. Is that understood?" I didn't agree to do what he said; I just walked out of the office.

I went back to class and sat quietly. I did the work she asked me to do. If there was something I didn't understand, I tried to figure it out to the best of my ability. I would never ask the teacher for help. I knew that if I asked for help, it would mean having to talk to her, and I didn't want to talk to anyone.

Then school was out and I went to the daycare center to pick up the three little kids. There was trash everywhere in the house when I walked in, as usual. Every day was the same. I didn't like living in my aunt's house, but I had nowhere else to go. Sometimes I would be too tired to eat supper because of doing so much cleaning.

One day, after picking up the kids from the daycare, I asked Robin if she could watch the children while I went to the store. But when I left, I went in the opposite direction. I finally came to the end of the projects. I could see three teenagers sitting on the concrete wall drinking beer and smoking marijuana. I walked past them. They didn't say anything to me, and I didn't say anything to them. Now I reached the next block, Washington Street. I continued to walk until I reached a one-way street. The cars here drove in the opposite direction of the cars on Washington. I read the sign: Jefferson Street.

The Church of God in Christ was on the corner of Jefferson Street. I looked at the church, walked alongside the building, and sat on the grass. While looking at the building and sitting in the grass I began to think this was God's house. I had never been to church before, yet I learned about God from my mother's friend Gail in Henderson, Nevada. She would always say, "Praise God." I remembered asking Gail who God was. She told me that I couldn't see Him, but He could hear me. If I called out to Him, He would answer my prayers. "And," she said, "Never forget God loves you."

I sat on the grass in front of the big dark orange church, hoping God would sit with me so I could ask Him to find me somewhere else to live. But I didn't hear from God. After a while I was tired of waiting to hear from Him. I got up and walked down Jefferson Street, not ready to go home. Thoughts of Maria came to my mind as I recalled how I felt at Child's Haven.

As I approached the corner, I saw a little corner store called Reddy's Corner. Across from Reddy's Corner was a park. I could see the kids playing from where I was standing.

When the light turned green, I crossed the street with the rest of the people going to the park. As I came closer I could read the name, Eastlake Park. I went inside the building. There were teenage boys playing basketball in the gym.

In the recreation area, the kids were playing ping-pong, badminton, and all kinds of games. I liked this place, and I knew I would be back. It was getting dark, so I turned to go home. I returned the same way I had come; it was easy.

When I reached the projects, I saw police cars and an ambulance. I thought about when Matthew was locked outside all night. Then I remembered that when I had stabbed Brad, there had been an ambulance. I walked past all the people. One lady was crying because someone had stabbed her son.

The police were asking everyone if they had seen anyone wearing a blue shirt and blue jeans. They were looking for a black male.

I walked faster to get home. I knew I would be in trouble for staying away for so long. When I got home, the kids were asking me where I'd been. I told them I'd been outside playing.

I went to the kitchen to get something to eat. Looking in the sink, I saw a pile of dirty dishes, so I went to the girls and asked whose turn it was to wash the dishes. All together, they told me it was my job to keep the house clean.

I felt like a slave on a plantation – the only difference was this plantation belonged to my aunt, uncle and her children instead of my mother and her boyfriend. I washed the dishes and went to bed. I was angry and did not eat anything.

⌒ THE NEXT MORNING ⌒

The next morning, Aunt Gina looked in the pantry and saw a pile of dirty clothes. She asked me why I hadn't washed the clothes. I didn't say anything, but it made me angry that she would ask when she had children who could help around the house. I continued to get the younger children ready for daycare.

I remember walking to school very upset. I went to my classroom and slammed my book on the desk.

The teacher asked me what was wrong. Without answering her, I knocked my books on the floor. She called the principal's office again.

This time the principal came to class to get me. He took me to his office and took out this big red paddle. He didn't ask any questions. He told me to place my hand on the back of a brown chair and face the wall. He swatted me twice and said he didn't want any more problems out of me. "Is that understood?" he asked.

I just looked at him. The paddle stung a little bit, but not enough to make me behave. I was angry and I didn't care who knew it.

I went back to class. Mrs. Tavlareadis asked me to read and I refused to do so. I sat in my chair rocking my foot back and forth. No one was going to make me do anything.

"Janice, do you understand what I'm asking you to do?" she asked. I looked at her, and then she told the kids they would be taking an early recess.

The kids went outside to play, the teacher pulled a chair up next to me. She told me she would be calling my mother concerning my behavior.

I said to her, "My mother is dead." Suddenly I jumped out of the chair and ran home, crying all the way. I sat bent over on the porch with my head between my knees. Crying, I looked up to the sky and called out to my mother, "I know you're in heaven. I know you can hear me."

Then I asked God, "Why did my mother have to die?"

My aunt walked up, sat beside me, and asked me to go inside the apartment with her. She told me my teacher had called her at her job, concerned about my behavior. She told me she understood that this was a painful time for me right now. Soon, she said, it would become easier to live without my mother. I was too afraid to tell her I didn't want to live with her anymore, so I listened to her so she would go back to work and leave me alone. I guess I really wasn't listening, because she asked me twice if I wanted to go in to take a nap. I said yes so she would leave.

I went in the house, lay down on the bed, and fell asleep. I was awakened by the noise of my aunt's children coming home from school.

Robin walked in and asked me where the three little kids were. I told her I was going to the daycare center to get them.

James and Ava were happy to see me as always. I was in a hurry, because I wanted to go back to that park I had found. I switched on the television and turned the channel to Sesame Street. Big Bird captured the kids' attention long enough for me to escape out the back door.

I walked the same way I had walked the first time. People were still drinking beer and smoking marijuana on the brick wall.

I went to the big church on the corner to see if I would hear from God. I peeked into the window, hoping to catch someone talking to God, but I didn't see anyone. I sat where I'd sat the last time and asked, "God, where are you?"

Someone tapped me on my shoulder. Chills went through my body. I was afraid to look up. I thought it was God. But the voice said, "Janice, come into the church. You are at the right place for help." The voice sounded familiar. When I turned to look, it was my principal. He was the pastor of this church. I asked him if he came to hear from God. He helped me up off the ground and we walked into the church.

We sat together in the front of the church. He said the same thing Gail said. God loved me and he heard me when I asked for something from Him. He told me that God was not in a hurry to answer me, but if I was a good girl at school, then God would take care of all my needs and some of the things I want the most. I promised to be good in school. I really wanted to ask God to take us back to Child Haven.
The pastor told me about the church and about Sunday School. When we finished talking he placed his hand on my head and talked to God for me. I felt much better.

I went home thinking about Sunday school. Washing clothes and doing the dishes were no big deal anymore. I was going to be good no matter what I had to do. I wanted to hear from God.

SEPTEMBER 1974

I'd done great last year. I'd graduated from fifth grade and was on my way to junior high. Booker T. Washington Junior High School was where I would be going to school in a few days.

My aunt had a new husband, half-white and half-black. His name was Charles. He reminded me of Santa Claus because he had a very long beard. Charles had an old truck that reminded me of Fred Sanford's truck on the television show "Sanford and Son", except Charles's truck was yellow.

One day Charles took us to meet his parents. Boy, I was amazed. His father was white and his mother was black. They were old and moved around the house slowly. I liked going to their house. When they knew we were coming, she would bake sweetbread. They were nice people and they were always happy to see us, all 11 of us.

Charles came from a big family of nine boys and one girl. The girl's name was Helen, and she was a very pretty lady with long black hair down her back. All of Charles's brothers looked like him and they all lived in beautiful homes.

It was the first day of school and I was excited, except for the painful knots I had in my chest. It hurt badly. I asked my teacher, Mrs. Myers, if I could go to the nurse's office because I was having pain in my chest. She gave me a pass to give to the nurse.

The nurse raised my right arm and put her hand where I told her I felt the pain. She said, "Sit down, dear, you're growing breasts." My surprise showed on my face. She nodded her head. "It won't last forever," she said, meaning the pain. I went back to class.

Now that I knew I was growing a breast, it was time to dress a little older. I began to wear my hair down and put on my aunt's makeup after she went to work. I would take it off before she came home from work. My jeans were a little tighter than normal.

Boys took a special interest in me. My hair was very long and I would twirl it to get them to carry my books from class to class.

Girls did not like the idea of their boyfriends following me around even if I didn't like the boys. I enjoyed flirting with them.

One day there was a big rumor that there would be a big fight after school at Eastlake Park. Many people knew about it at school.

On my way home I was walking with some of my guy friends. Matthew had told us that the girls were walking together on the other side of the street because they were going to fight me once we made it to the park. I started braiding my hair. I didn't want my hair to get pulled. I was not afraid to fight. In my house, fistfighting was a way of life with 11 children in the home.

However, I did not like the idea of five girls fighting me at one time. I asked Matthew who I was supposed to be fighting. He said, "Bernice." I told him to go across the street and tell them I would fight them all, but one at a time and on different days. Bernice sent back the message that she was going to whip my butt as soon as I stepped on the grass at the park. Barbara said she would fight me the following day.

I stepped in the grass at the park and Bernice started swinging at me before I could even get my coat off. She pulled my hair as we tossed and turned in the grass. I managed to get on top of her and began to hit her in her face. The men who worked at the recreation center came and broke up the fight.

Bernice and her friends went across the street yelling and cussing, saying it wasn't over and telling me not to come to school tomorrow.

I made it home and the police were everywhere as usual. This time they were taking people to jail because of a shooting of a Crip gang member. Charles told us to go into the house. He was tired of all the killings and shootings in the projects.

I looked at my sister. She had very short hair. Her hair had been cut. This really made me mad. I thought to myself, "She cut my baby sister's hair off because her girls don't have any hair." I started looking for my aunt to ask her why she cut Ava's hair off. She was in her room talking to Charles. I knocked on the door and asked her why she cut Ava's hair. She told me it was too long. I couldn't believe it. Ava looked like a little boy.

Everybody in the house was more concerned about the gunshots that continued to ring out throughout the projects. I was concerned about my sister's hair. I watched my little sister play as if she didn't notice her hair was gone, listened to the gunshots, and wished I could go back to Child Haven.

The gunshots went on all night. We were told to lie down in our beds in case a bullet came through a window. I heard Charles tell Aunt Gina he'd had enough and we would be moving out of the projects.

The gunshots rang out so loud the sounds seemed to come from right outside our window. This scared me, making it hard for me to sleep. I cuddled next to my baby sister, hoping she wouldn't be awakened by the gunshots. I knew if she woke up it would be hard for me to get her back to sleep. Somewhere between the gunshots, tossing, and turning all night, I fell asleep.

For the next week, the fighting after school continued, at least until I had beaten up enough girls to convince them I was not a coward. My grades were still good, considering all the work I had to do at home and the fights I was in after school. With cleaning and caring for the three little children, I would get to bed late. Some mornings I would be so tired I would fall asleep in class. Mrs. Myers told me he would be calling my house if I didn't start going to bed early. I didn't want her to call my aunt, and I learned to manage my time and get to bed at a decent hour.

One day I was hanging clothes on the clothesline and a black lady with two girls walked up to me. "Is Gina in the house?" she asked. I told her I would go into the house to get her.

Aunt Gina came out behind me. My aunt and the lady talked for a moment, then Aunt Gina introduced me to the lady. "Janice, this is Roxanne. Her daughters are your stepsisters, your father's children," she explained.

Aunt Gina would not allow my sisters to visit in her house. I thought this was mean, to have to visit outside. One of the girls looked like me, with black curly hair. The other one had a light complexion with red hair. Roxanne promised to always bring the girls to see me. She didn't keep her promise.

I had begun to wonder what my father looked like. I remembered spending a lot of time with him, his teaching me how to use the potty by myself. I would make it to the potty-chair too late. He'd potty-trained me at the home of a Ms. Washington. After Roxanne left, I asked Aunt Gina where my father was. She told me he had died somewhere in California shortly after my mother did. She didn't know exactly where.

CHAPTER 5

⌒ SOUTHERN PHOENIX ⌒

My aunt and Charles started bringing boxes home for us to pack our belongings in. They had bought a house in Southern Phoenix. I was very happy to be moving out of the projects.

This house had five bedrooms and two bathrooms, a front yard, and a huge back yard. It was green with yellow trim around the top edge of the house. The boys had two bedrooms and so did the girls. The kitchen was big, but the living room was small.

We all started school the next day. The school I attended was Percy L. Julian Junior High School. The three little kids were in school across the street. I would pick them up after school was out each day.

I liked Percy L. Julian Middle School. I learned how to play softball and tried out for the softball team. I made the team and the girls on the team were nice. They were nothing like the girls at the school in the projects. These girls weren't jealous of each other. In the morning, they would help each other put their makeup on and change their hairstyles from the way their mothers had fixed it. I thought I was the only one who took her mother's makeup to school and put it on at school. We would all take off the makeup before we went home. Sometimes I would forget, but my aunt never paid attention to me or to what was going on in my life.

I was in eighth grade now; the teachers were preparing us for high school.

There was a book contest going on in the library. The library teacher's name was Mrs. James. She told us the contest would be for the student who reads the most books and does a book report on all the books. At the end of the school year the student who had read the most books would receive a scholarship to the high school of his or her choice.

I entered the book contest. I started in 50th place because I'd found out about the contest two days late.

I was determined to win this contest. I read books on famous people, such as Harriet Tubman, Joe Namath, Jackie Robinson, and John Denver. I wrote my book reports on who they were and how they became famous.

I became obsessed with reading, not because I wanted to win the scholarship, but because the librarian had taken a special interest in what I was doing. Every day Mrs. James would ask me about the next person I was reading about. I started spending a tremendous amount of time with her after school.

I asked my cousin Caron if she would walk the three little kids home from school for me so I could win this contest. She did it for the rest of the school year. This made it easier for me to read more books.

I finally reached first place; the hard work had started to pay off. I needed to stay in first place in order to win. Being in first place was awesome. I cannot find the words to express the way I felt the day I walked in the library and saw a gold star by my name. No one had ever made me feel as important as my library teacher did before and during that contest.

Mrs. James lived a block from the school. I would go to her house after school and sometimes on the weekends. I enjoyed being with her and she liked having me around.

At the end of the school year, I had won the Librarian's Award Scholarship. I'd read 103 books.

I went home to tell my aunt and asked her if I could attend high school at North Phoenix High. She said no. I stood next to her bed waiting for an explanation as to why I couldn't go to that particular school.

"Get out of my room," she said. I dropped my head and told myself I couldn't take any more of this. Nothing I did was good enough for anyone in this house.

I went to the living room. My brother was rocking back and forth on the couch as if he had a nervous condition. I sat next to him and put my hand on his belly to stop him from rocking. He would stop for a moment then begin rocking again. He had found comfort in rocking back and forth until he rocked himself to sleep. I laid his head in my lap as I thought of a way to run away from this house. I'd better wait until graduation, I thought. Maybe my aunt would change her mind about allowing me to go to North Phoenix High School.

JUNE 1976 – GRADUATION

Everyone was excited about graduation. I still had hope that my aunt would change her mind.

The principal decided we would have our graduation in the auditorium at South Mountain High. We tried on our robes; they were maroon and gold, our school colors.

All the students were deciding which school they would like to attend. I wanted to go to North Phoenix High School, because there weren't a lot of fights there. The school closest to our house was South Mountain High. From what people said about it, South was just like Booker T. Washington, my old junior high school.

The day before graduation I started my menstruation. I was so afraid. I didn't know why I had blood coming out of my private area. I put toilet paper in my underwear, not wanting to mess up my underclothes. I took the bloody tissue to my aunt to show her that I was bleeding down there. She said, "Girl, close my bedroom door."

My heart dropped. I didn't know what to do or think. I went to the back room and told Robin. She said, "Girl, that is natural, just like you grew those breasts. This is another part of you changing into a teenager." I asked her if it had happened to her yet. She said yes. But her mother was there for her because she'd been as afraid as I was.

I left the room, but I was certain about one thing. Living here was just a way to have a roof over my head. I thought about my mother not being here for me when I needed her the most. I became very angry, and there was no church down the street for me to visit to talk to God.

I walked outside and my friend next door, Sonya, was standing at her gate. "Janice, what's wrong?" she asked. I told her, "My life." I really didn't feel like talking. I told her I was going for a walk. "It's getting dark," she said. I told her I didn't care.

I saw lights across the field where the cows were. I asked Sonya what the big bright lights were. She told me it was a park called Hermosa. I told her I was going to walk in the direction of those lights. If I got to the park, I planned to be there for about an hour. I needed time to myself. Sonya told me to be careful, Hermosa Park was not the best park in the world. I really didn't care; anything was better than where I lived.

As I walked toward the lights, I came to a dead-end street, and at the end of the street I saw that I could get into the park. The bright lights were for the people playing softball on the field.

I thought to myself that maybe I would watch the softball game. I loved softball. As I got closer to the game, I saw the players were girls who appeared to be my age, some maybe a little older. I sat and watched the game. Both teams were good.

Later I searched for the restroom and noticed that Hermosa Park was just like Eastlake Park near the projects. The only difference was that this park was a lot cleaner. After I came out of the restroom, I asked the man working in the supply office if I could play softball. He told me to fill out an application and take it to my parents to sign.

"Why do my parents have to sign?" I asked. He said it was so the park wouldn't have to pay if I was injured. I knew I wouldn't be able to play, because I knew my aunt was not going to sign anything that made me happy. She was never interested in anything I did except my cleaning her house, washing the clothes, and taking care of the kids. I only had her attention if one of those things was not completed.

"What's wrong?" he asked. "Nothing. I was just thinking," I replied. He told me to have it back to the recreation office by the first week of June. When I walked outside the softball game was over.

It was late when I started walking home. Two guys and a girl I knew who lived behind me asked me if I wanted to walk with them. The girl's name was Bonnie. She had played on one of the teams that night. Tom and Henry were her next-door neighbors. Their job was to walk her home after the game. I told Bonnie that I was interested in playing softball in the summer. She asked if I had gotten the application to play. I told her I had it, but that I didn't think my aunt would allow me to play.
"Why?" Bonnie asked. "It's a long story," I replied.

They walked me home and went around the corner. Before Bonnie left, she gave me her telephone number.

I walked in the house, and my aunt asked me where I had been. I told her I had been down the street at my friend's house.

"Get in there and wash those dishes," she demanded. I didn't care because I was used to it.

After I washed the dishes, I went to her room and asked her if she was coming to my graduation tomorrow. "You graduate to-morrow, Janice?" she asked with surprise. I said yes.

"Well, I knew it was soon, but I didn't think it was tomorrow. I'm sorry. I can't make it," she explained. I walked out of the room and sat on the couch thinking. I had nothing new to wear to my graduation. I knew my classmates would make fun of me tomorrow, just as they had at Christmastime.

Last year at Christmastime, the teacher had asked us to draw names out of a hat. We were to buy a Christmas gift for the person whose name we pulled out of the hat. I didn't want to participate. I knew my aunt was not going to give me any money. The week we were to exchange gifts, I looked around the house for something to give my classmate.

I had drawn a girl named Tina. She was very popular at school. At home, I had found a broken gold-gilded chain and a box. I took red crayons and colored the inside of the box.

The day we'd exchanged gifts, Tina was the first name called. I'd given her the box and she had opened it and yelled, "What the hell is this?" She had raised it high in the air so my classmates could see. When they'd started laughing, I jumped out of my seat and ran outside the room. I sat outside the classroom door, listening to them laugh and make fun of the chain.

The teacher had come outside. "Don't cry, Janice," he'd said.

"My family is poor. We don't have money, or I would have bought her something new," I'd explained to him. He'd told me to tell Tina that. He went back into the classroom, and Tina came out.

"I couldn't buy you anything from a store because my family is very poor. We share each other's shoes. It's 11 kids in our home. I knew my aunt wouldn't give me money, so I gave you what I had found. I'm sorry," I explained. Tina had hugged me and said it was OK.

When we walked back into the classroom, Tina had told them not to laugh because I'd given her what I had to give, and it came from my heart. Then she'd turned and looked toward me and said, "Thank you." The class had clapped their hands and apologized.

As I sat on the couch thinking about that incident, a few tears rolled down my face. I knew they would laugh again tomorrow at graduation.

I got up and went to my room looking in my dresser for something to wear. All I owned were jeans and tennis shoes.

I went to Robin to ask if she had something I could wear to my graduation. She told me to look in her closet. I took out a blue dress, and she also allowed me to wear her black shoes.

I felt a sense of relief. I had something nice to wear. I put the clothes on my dresser and took a shower. As I was coming out of the shower, Robin said, "Have a good time tomorrow." I said thank you and went to bed.

I woke up early for school that morning. I was so excited. I was going to graduate today! Graduation was a big deal to me, but not to anyone else in the house. It was just another day to them. No one else seemed to care.

I was not going to allow them to spoil this day for me.

I left for school early. On the way to school I saw Bonnie. "Hi," she said. I asked her if she was going to school at Julian. She told me she was going to attend South Mountain. I told her I might be attending that school next year. She wanted to know if I was going to the park tonight. If I was, she would swing by to get me. I needed to be ready by 4:30. Her softball game was at 5:30. I told her I would be ready, and she left to catch her bus.

When I arrived at school, all the students were getting ready for graduation.

The bell rang and the teacher began taking roll call as usual. We lined up one more time to practice our march. Everyone was happy and talking about the school year.

The principal came to our classroom door and told us we were next on the bus.

The bus arrived at South Mountain High School. This was a big school. The teenagers looked much older than we did. The bus driver drove slowly through the campus. Anxiously, we waited for the teachers to recount us before we exited the bus.

One by one, our teacher handed us our robes as we stepped off the bus. I was amazed at how huge and round the auditorium was. When we walked in, the lights were bright and beautiful. On the stage was the band from South High, looking neat and well organized.

Our teacher directed us to our seats. A few minutes later our principal walked onstage. The auditorium became silent. The principal began his speech of congratulations to the graduates. Then it was time for the awards.

I watched our library teacher, Mrs. James, as she walked across the stage. My heart started racing fast. I knew I was next to receive my scholarship. Mrs. James said many nice things about me, things I had never heard anyone say about me. When she called my name, the whole class stood up, clapping their hands as I moved across the seats and walked down the aisle. I finally made it to the stage without falling. I was so nervous. I thought for sure I would fall. Mrs. James handed me the scholarship and shook my hand. She pointed at the microphone.

I was so nervous I forgot my speech. I'd left it on my seat. "First of all, I would like to thank my library teacher for believing in me and giving me encouragement when I could not find the courage to go on. I would also like to thank my classmates for accepting me as I am," I said gratefully.

After all the awards ceremonies, we received our diplomas one by one to the sound of "Pomp and Circumstance." We marched outside on the count of three; we threw our hats up in the air. Everyone started hugging each other.

The teacher counted us as we boarded the bus. We laughed and talked all the way back to school. This was one of the best days of my life. I will never forget it.

～ LATER THAT EVENING ～

After graduation, I went home to show everyone my diploma. But nobody cared. I wanted them to be proud of me.

I walked down to the corner house. The lady who lived there was named Pearl. She opened the door and told me to come back after her husband left. I said "OK" and walked away swiftly. I understood why she said it. Her husband was a mean man who beat her often. Several times, the beatings were so bad she ended up in the hospital for days.

Since nobody was interested in seeing my diploma, I took it and threw it in the bottom drawer of my dresser. I went to the living room and began watching television until Bonnie came to get me.

My cousin Alicia asked me where I was going. I told her I was going to the store. She told me she would tell her mother if I left the house. I didn't care. I'd had enough of them and the way they treated me.

Bonnie and I walked to the park. I told her I was thinking about leaving home now that school was out. She wanted to know where I was going to go. I told her I didn't know. By the time we reached the park, Bonnie knew almost my whole life story. She understood why I couldn't take living there any longer.

She asked me if I'd brought the permission slip to play softball. I told her I had the paper in my pocket. She asked for it and I gave it to her.

"What's your aunt's name?" she asked. I told her, and she signed my aunt's name on the application. I turned it in to the recreation center; the man working there took it.

Bonnie's team lost the game this time. While we were walking home, I could tell she didn't care for losing. I tried to talk about something else to take her mind off the game. She laughed and said, "I like hanging out with you, Janice." I replied, "I like hanging out with Janice too." We started laughing together.

Bonnie wrote her telephone number on a piece of paper and gave it to me a second time. She told me to call her if I needed to talk. The back yard of her house was right behind mine, across the valley.

When I returned home, my aunt was yelling because I hadn't washed the dishes. I didn't say anything; I walked to my room.

A few minutes later my aunt was standing in the door of my room. "Go wash the dishes," she said.

"With all these people in this house, why do I still have to wash their dishes and their clothes?" I asked.

"Just do what you are told to do," she demanded, and walked away.

I went to the kitchen and did the dishes. Afterward, I sat outside under the car porch thinking of a way to move out of the house. As I sat there, the same question kept coming into my head: "Where are you going to go?"

I didn't have the slightest idea. The traffic in front my house had slowed down; I knew it was getting late. I walked into the house and turned off the TV. When I passed my aunt's bedroom, I saw she was sound asleep. She didn't know I had been out of the house almost three hours. I told myself, "She would make it so easy to leave here. If only I could find somewhere else to live."

SUMMER 1976

Bonnie and I went to the park every day. I had joined the softball team. We were also at the park when there were no softball games.

Boys were there. I liked a boy named George. He was tall with a light brown complexion and long dark black hair.

I was hardly at home and no one seemed to notice. I spent more time with George. When I was with George, we had fun. We would meet at the park and go walking to the store, or watch television at his house. If we didn't have a softball game, Bonnie would meet me at the park by 8:00 p.m. From there we would walk home together.

One night George and I were sitting on the bench at the park. School was starting in two weeks. George would be a junior, while I was only a freshman in high school. George had attended South High last year.

While we were sitting on the bench talking, an ambulance and fire trucks drove swiftly past the park. The ambulance made a left at the light, another left at the next light, and stopped. I stood up. "What's wrong?" George asked. "The ambulance stopped close to my house," I said.

Bonnie came running. "Janice, let's go see what happened," she said, out of breath. George said he would walk with us.

We walked down the dead-end street and turned right. The rest of the street was sectioned off with yellow tape. The police would not allow cars to drive through. They allowed us to walk on the sidewalk if we lived in one of the houses on the block.

All the neighbors were standing outside watching. I asked Sonya what had happened. She told me that Jesse, Pearl's husband, had beat Pearl for the last time. I asked her what she meant. "Jesse came home from work and beat Pearl up. In the process of him hitting her, she grabbed the shotgun from under the bed and shot him," Sonya explained.

My mouth fell open. I could not imagine Pearl with a gun. Sonya went on to say, "The street is blocked because Jesse died in the house."

"Wow!" I said in amazement. This took me back to my mother's boyfriend killing her. "Are you OK?" George asked me. I nodded my head yes. Bonnie knew where I had gone in my head. She grabbed my hand and said that not all parents kill each other. "Well, that's kind of hard to believe," I said angrily.

I asked Sonya where Pearl was. She told me they had taken Pearl to jail. "What about the kids?" I asked. Sonya said their grandmother picked them up and took them with her.

I saw my cousins walking toward us and slipped my hand out of George's. I didn't want to give my cousins anything to go tell their mother.

Everyone stood outside watching as the ambulance and fire trucks pulled away. There were mixed opinions concerning the incident. Some neighbors said Jesse got what he deserved, and others said Pearl didn't have to kill him. I didn't know what to feel. My feelings were different, because I know what it is like to have a parent taken away by another parent, only to lose both parents.

The only cars left were two police cars and a white car that said CORONER. Sonya's father told us that the coroner was the person who pronounced a person dead. The coroner was still outside when everybody went back into their homes.

A WEEK LATER

My aunt went to work as usual. I fixed cereal and washed the dishes after everyone had eaten.

About 10:00 a.m. Sonya came to the door. She said she'd seen Pearl walk into her house. I didn't believe her.
"Janice, you're her friend, go see," Sonya said anxiously. I told her I would go in the house and call.

I dialed the number. A soft vice answered, "Hello." I didn't know if I should hang up or speak. The voice continued to say hello, then the telephone went dead. Whoever answered the telephone had hung up.

I called back. "Hello," said the voice answering the telephone. "Pearl, it's me, Janice," I said. She asked if I was at home, and if I could please come down there.

I was scared. She sounded like she needed me. I put my shoes on, walked to her house and rang the doorbell. She peeped out the window and opened the door. She asked me to sit down. When she sat next to me, I told her she didn't have to tell me anything. I only wanted to know if there was anything I could do for her.

It was quiet for a long minute. She began to cry. "I couldn't take it anymore. I didn't mean to kill him, but it was either him or me," she explained.

I didn't say anything. I watched her as she wiped the tears from her eyes. In some strange way, I was happy she'd lived to be here with her children.

We heard her mother's key in the door. I stood up and said I was leaving. Pearl asked me to stay a little while longer, but I told her she should be with her mother. I opened the door and left.

CHAPTER 6

 SEPTEMBER 1976

It was the first day of school and students were already calling me "dumb freshman" because I looked lost. I couldn't find my classes. And George was supposed to meet me. He'd promised to carry my books to all my classes. I stood in front of the cafeteria waiting for him.

"Janice," I heard someone call. It sounded like Bonnie. I looked back and saw Bonnie waving her hand, motioning for me to come over. She looked so anxious. I walked toward her swiftly.
"What do you want?" I asked. She told me to come with her because she needed to show me something.

We walked to the back of the school, and there was George, on his knees shooting dice for money. I tapped him on the shoulder. "What do you think you're doing?" I asked. He was surprised to see me. "I...I...I..." he stuttered.

I walked away. He grabbed his money and followed me, trying to explain why he was gambling. I walked faster, looking for my class. "Will you listen to me?" he asked. I opened the classroom door and went in.

The teacher asked me if I was Janice Higgins. I nodded my head yes and sat in the first open desk I saw.

I looked out the window to see George. I did see him, and he was not going to class. He just hung out around my classroom door. I seethed inside with anger. I kept saying to myself, "He really is not going to class."

I don't remember hearing a word the teacher said in class, but I sure heard the bell ring.

I walked outside. Bonnie and George were standing there. I told Bonnie I would meet her for lunch in the cafeteria.

As we walked to my next class, I asked George why he wasn't going to class. He told me he wouldn't get in trouble for missing one class. Besides, he said that he wanted to talk to me. I told him we could talk after school. He asked, "What about lunchtime?" I told him I was meeting Bonnie for lunch. He looked angry as he walked away.

The bell rang and George was again waiting outside the door of my classroom. He walked me to every class until lunch. We walked to the cafeteria together. I told him I would see him later and went to the table where Bonnie was waiting for me.

"Girl, I wanted to tell you about George when you first started seeing him. George is into many things. I remember him talking to many girls. But when I saw he was with you all the time, I didn't see him with anyone else," she explained.
"What do you mean a lot of things?" I asked. "Well, shooting dice, drinking and not going to class," she said.

The bell rang. I told Bonnie I wouldn't be meeting her after school. I needed to talk to George. She asked me not to tell him what we had discussed. I promised her I wouldn't.

After school, George and I took the bus down Southern Ave. We went to the park to talk and sat in the grass.
"So tell me about yourself. I don't want to have any more surprises," I said. He told me there was nothing else to tell. I knew he was lying and I asked him to walk me halfway home.

"Why are you leaving so early?" he asked. I told him I had homework and asked him where his was. He said he'd left his books in his locker at school.

"That's not going to help," I said. He asked me if we could do our homework together tomorrow. "Sure," I said with a smile.

1978

Things were the same all year. I had an after-school job now. I didn't get to spend much time with George, and I hardly saw Bonnie. I looked forward to seeing George at school, that didn't change. He still walked me to all my classes.

One morning I looked for him and he was nowhere to be found. I went around the back of the school to see if he was in the back shooting dice. He wasn't there, and no one had seen him. I didn't see him at all that day in school.

I called my job to tell them I wouldn't be in and took the bus straight home. I called George's house; there was no answer. I walked to the park, but still no one had seen him.

I went back home to call his house again. Still, no one answered the telephone. I tossed and turned all night. It was not like him to be away from me without calling. Every time I heard the phone ring I jumped out of bed, hoping it was him. The night turned into morning, and still I had not heard from George.

THE NEXT MORNING

The next morning students came to me saying, "I'm sorry about what happened to George." I didn't have a clue what they were talking about.

Tony, a friend of George, sat down next to me in the cafeteria during lunch. He said, "The girl died, huh?" I looked at him with a confused expression on my face and asked, "What are you talking about?"

He replied, "George – oh, you don't know what happened yesterday? He was on top of the house cleaning a gun, and when it went off, it shot a little girl in the head. She was sitting in front of her school."

I started screaming and crying. They had to take me to the principal's office. My stomach felt like there were a million knots in it. I felt as if I wanted to throw up, but couldn't. The principal called my aunt at work, and she told them to allow me to go home. I cried myself to sleep.

My aunt woke me when she came home from work. She was upset because she hadn't known I had a boyfriend. Especially one that played with guns.

She became more upset when I wouldn't talk to her. I felt she had never taken an interest in what was going on in my life, so why should she bother now?

"Here he is in the newspaper. Due to him being a minor, he will get out of juvenile hall in six months. I don't want you to ever see him again. Do you understand?" she said. I didn't say anything. I just looked at her. She walked out of the room and told everybody in the house my boyfriend was a murderer. This really made me angry. She told my cousins that if they saw me with him after they let him out, they were to tell her and she would whip my butt.

I followed her, looking to see where she was going to put the newspaper. I wanted to read it. She took it to her room.

I called Bonnie to ask her if she'd heard about what George had done. She told me everybody knew. "It's been on television and in the newspapers since yesterday," she explained. She didn't want to be the one to always bring me bad news about my boyfriend. Bonnie asked how I'd found out about George. I told her Tony had told me during lunch. I could not believe it.

I also told her my aunt had the paper and that she'd found out he was my boyfriend from the principal. I asked Bonnie how I could get that article from the newspaper. She told me she had one and would cut out the article and bring it to me in about 20 minutes.

I didn't know what to do. I stared out the living room window, watching the cows in the field.

I thought about how much pain the little girl's parents must be in. Although it was an accident, that didn't take away the pain they must be feeling. George's parents are very nice people. I couldn't help but wonder how they felt about what happened to their son and what he did. Now I understood why they hadn't been answering the telephone when I'd called the other day.

I saw Bonnie coming while I was in the window and met her on the sidewalk. She handed me the newspaper article. I started reading it as we walked.

"Wow," I said after reading the article. "He really killed someone." Bonnie said it was an accident. I looked at her. "Anytime a person is playing or cleaning a loaded gun, you take the risk of someone getting hurt," I explained.

"He didn't know the gun was loaded, he was only cleaning it," she said in his defense. "Well, somebody thinks he was wrong. He's in juvenile hall," I stated.

"Did you read the paper correctly? He's in juvenile hall for cleaning a gun in a residential area. If the police didn't believe it was an accident, he would be in juvenile hall for longer than six months," she explained.

She asked me how I felt. "I just feel," I said. We made it to the park; I looked around and began to cry. Things appeared so different without George.

"Are you going to be with him when he comes home from juvenile hall?" asked Bonnie. I told her I didn't know, but that one thing was for sure: my aunt was going to make sure I stayed away from him. We didn't stay at the park long; Bonnie had homework to do, so we left.

⌒ SIX MONTHS LATER ⌒

One evening while I was watching television the telephone rang. I said, "Hello." The voice on the other end of the phone said, "I miss you."

"George," I whispered. "Yes, it's me," he said quietly.

"You can't call here. My aunt knows what happened to you and what you did. She told me I'm not allowed to see you ever again," I explained.

"Could you meet me at the park in 30 minutes? After we talk, you will never have to see me again. If you don't want to, OK," he said. I agreed to meet him at the park.

I called Bonnie's house, wanting her to walk with me, but she wasn't home. I had never walked to the park alone. Today would be the first time. I left the house without telling anyone as usual.

I arrived at the park, but I didn't see George. As I walked to the end of the park nearest his house, I saw him coming.

He approached me and hugged me. I didn't hug him back. I didn't know if I should hug him. He kept asking me what was wrong. I told him I didn't think we should see each other anymore.

"But I love you. Don't you love me?" he asked. He had never said that before. I told him I loved him.

"If you do," he said, "then prove it." I asked him how I was supposed to prove I loved him. He asked me to go to his house. I told him I couldn't. I had to be at work at Burger King in a few hours.

"If you loved me, you would show me," he said repeatedly. I told him I would go to his house tomorrow.

"Before I went to juvenile hall, we went everywhere together, and now you don't want to go to my house. Are you seeing someone else?" he said angrily. I had never heard him talk this way. He was being very demanding. I told him I was going home and turned to walk away.

He grabbed my arm and said, "We've been hanging out a year and half now. You're doing what everybody else is doing to me. I made one mistake and now I'm the villain. How in the hell can your aunt tell you to stay away from me? I'm the one who bought you new school clothes when your aunt gave you her kids' hand-me-down clothes and their run-down shoes. Do you remember that? Janice, you're my girl, and I need you right now to just be the friend you've always been," he finished with a sad look on his face.

He made me cry. In my heart I wanted to be with him. Yet I didn't want to get in trouble at home and I explained this to him. He told me that if I kept my job, and he got a job, we could move in together. That was exactly what I wanted to do, move out of my aunt's house. We agreed to save our money and look for an apartment.

He walked me halfway home. I kissed him good-bye and told him I would call him when I got off work at 10:00 p.m. And I told him to make sure the telephone was in his room.

I went home and got ready for work. I had never been so happy. I was finally going to move out of this place. I walked past my aunt's room and looked inside to see her lying in bed reading a book. I wondered if she had ever told her own kids she loved them. I knew I'd never seen her hug them.

"Janice, what are you doing?" she asked. "I'm getting ready for work," I answered.

"Could you bring me a cup of water before you go?" she asked. "Sure," I said, and went to get the water. When I took it to her, she looked sick. I asked her what was wrong. She told me she was having a baby.

"Another one?" I said with surprise in my eyes. "Well, Charles wants a baby," she said. I walked out of the room saying to myself, I not taking care of another child. I left to catch the bus for work.

Burger King was a cool job. I ate everything in sight. This fat guy named Ted offered to take me home. Ted was a nice guy and I agreed to ride home with him on the nights we worked together. He didn't live far from me.

After we got off work, Ted asked me if I knew how to drive a car. I told him no.

"This Saturday I'll teach you how to drive. On your days off from work, you can catch the bus and come get the car," he said. I didn't say anything, because I didn't believe he was going to allow me to drive his car. I planned to wait until Saturday to see if he was telling the truth.

Ted dropped me off in front of the house. I told him I would see him tomorrow. He gave me his telephone number and told me to call if I needed anything at all.

When I walked into the house, everyone was in their rooms. I went to the back room to see who was up. I wanted to call George, and I didn't want anyone to know.

I took a shower and washed the dishes. Then I went to the living room to call George.

"Hello, I've been waiting for you to call," he said when he answered the telephone. "I had to wait until everyone was asleep," I explained.

"Remember, you promised to come to my house tomorrow," he said. I asked him why he was being so persistent about my coming to his house. "I miss you, that's all," he said sadly. I told him to meet me at the park at noon. He asked why I was getting off the telephone. I told him I was tired and we said good night.

THE NEXT DAY

George called at 9:00 a.m. He wanted to go to Christown Theater to see a movie, but I told him I wasn't up to it. I asked him if we could just watch television at his house.

I left my house at 11:30 a.m. When I got to the corner, I could see George coming. He had something behind his back. He'd picked some ugly flowers and he gave them to me. I said they were pretty; I didn't want to hurt his feelings. He smiled as he gave them to me.

When we made it to his house, I asked him where his parents were. "At work," he replied. We went into his room and he turned on the television. I took off my shoes.

George started rubbing his hands on my back. He unsnapped my bra. I asked him what he was doing as he unfastened my bra.

"You promised to show me you loved me today," he said. "But I didn't say I would take off my bra," I said, grabbing his hands. George wanted to have sex, and it took me by surprise.

We had always kissed and hugged, but we never talked about actually having sex. We played around with how many kids we were going to have when we got married. But it was all joking around.

We sat up and started talking about sex. He knew I had never done anything like this. I thought he had never done anything like this, until he told me he'd had a girlfriend before me. I asked him why he hadn't said anything before now.

"I didn't want to pressure you," he said. He didn't want to wait until we moved in together either. It was now or never. I didn't know what to do. I loved him very much and I didn't want to lose my boyfriend. So I agreed to have sex with him.

We lay in the bed talking for about an hour. He took my shirt off and unsnapped my bra. A certain part of me wanted him as much as he wanted me.

He moved his hands slowly across my breast. I watched him closely, wondering what he would do next. He continued to kiss me softly. I was nervous; he kept telling me to relax. I watched him as he climbed on top of me, taking off my panties with one hand.

Something inside me said, this is wrong, stop him. But I had gone this far, so I felt I might as well continue.

I felt him penetrate me. It was painful. I started pushing him away from me, my hands on his waist. It was too painful.

"I can't do this. It hurts, George, stop!" I said. I felt something rip and looked down to see blood on the sheets. I was scared. He had done something wrong to me. "Get off me!" I cried, pushing him away. He got up and said he was sorry. He tried to explain that the first time is supposed to hurt a little. I went to the restroom and washed up.

When I opened the door of the restroom, he was standing there. He hugged me. I watched him as he took the sheets off the bed; he put them in a plastic trash bag, then took them outside to the trash can.

I sat on his bed, crying softly. Something inside me said I shouldn't have done that. I felt different.

George walked back in the room and sat down beside me. He talked about us finding an apartment of our own to get me out of my aunt's house. I heard him, but I really didn't hear him. I was still in shock from what had just taken place.

He opened the door to his bedroom because he knew his parents would be coming home. We weren't allowed to be in his room with the door closed.

George turned the television to cartoons. I was quiet and did not say anything. He asked me if I was hungry. I told him no. "Well, I'm going to walk to OK's hamburger stand and get us some hamburgers. Do you want to walk with me?" he asked. "No," I said and lay down on the bed.

I felt weak and extremely tired. I got up to go to the kitchen to get a drink of water. My legs felt like I had just gotten off a horse. I walked funny, and it felt different. I went to the bathroom connected to his room and pulled down my pants and panties to see if I was still bleeding down there. It was not as bad as I thought. It was only a little blood. This made me feel better.

George came back with hamburgers and French fries. Every five minutes he would ask me if I was alright. I kept telling him I was OK. We watched television while eating our food.

I told George I needed to go home and get dressed for work. He wanted me to stay with him longer. "No, I have to go to work," I said.

He went in the other room to get the telephone. "What's the number to your job?" he asked. I told him. He called Burger World and told them I was sick and would not be in tonight. He told me my boss said he hoped I feel better.

"George, you are going to make me lose my job. Then we'll never get a place of our own," I said. "Don't worry. People call in sick all the time," he said.

He made another telephone call, this time to his friend. He said, "Come with me. My friend is going to let me use his car to take you to the movies."

"I don't want to go to the movies, I just want to lie down and watch television," I said.

"My mother and father will be home from work and I don't want them to think we've been here all day by ourselves. So come with me," he urged. I said "OK" and got up off the bed. We walked about two blocks to his friend's house. His friend gave him the keys to his car and told him to bring it back the next afternoon.

I was surprised. I hadn't known George knew how to drive. "Where are we going?" I asked. He said, "Just ride with me."

He stopped at the house of everyone he knew in the neighborhood to show them he could drive. After a while I was tired of riding around. I asked him to take me home. He asked me why. I told him I was tired and wanted to lie down.

George drove to the east side of Phoenix and pulled into the 7-11 parking lot. "Do you want anything out of the store?" he asked. I shook my head. He came out of the store with a bag of chips and sodas.

He drove down the street and pulled into Motel 6. I asked him what he was doing. "You want to lay down and watch television, don't you?" he asked. "Well, this is the only place that we can go to be together, and now you can lay down and watch all the television you want in one night."

I had never been in a motel before. I looked at him and wondered if he had.

"You come here often?" I asked. "Why would you ask that?" he responded.

"I've learned more about you in one day than in the whole year and a half I've known you," I said.

"I do things that older people do because I'm 18, and now that you've shown me you love me, I feel comfortable doing different things around you," he explained.

I watched him go to the motel window, fill out a piece of paper, and hand them some money. In return they gave him a key to a motel room. Room 222.

He turned on the lights and told me to come in. I entered the motel room and sat on the bed. Reaching for the remote control, I turned on the television. George told me to kick back and pretend we were in our own apartment for one night. When he said it like that, it made it easier for me to be in a motel with him.

I took my shoes and pants off. I pulled the covers back on the bed. I fluffed the pillows. They smelled fresh and clean. As I rested my head on the pillows, I remember saying to myself, "I could sleep here forever."

George was on the telephone calling all his friends, telling them he was in a motel with his girlfriend. As if he had never been there before. This made me think he didn't want me to know this was his first time in a motel. I could tell by the conversations he had with his friends on the telephone.

We started kissing and hugging again. George pulled off my shirt and got in bed with no clothes on. I was not as afraid as I had been the first time. When he penetrated me this time, it was not as painful as the first time. But it still hurt. I guessed the worst was over.

When he finished, I still didn't know what to feel. He went to the bathroom to wet a towel, came back, and wiped me off. There was still a little blood. He told me this was normal.

We put our clothes on. George went to the store to get some cards so we could play war. He returned a few minutes later and I was asleep. "Please let me sleep. I promise, I will play cards with you later," I said as I fell asleep.

I woke a couple of hours later. George was not in the room. I went to the restroom.

There was a clock on the television. It said 9:00 p.m. I knew I needed to be home by 10:30 so my aunt would think I was at work. I wondered where George had gone.

The telephone rang. It was George. "Why did you leave me here by myself?" I asked. He said he'd gone to get gas and clean clothes to put on in the morning. He was on his way back to the motel and wanted to know if I needed anything. "I can't stay here until morning." I said to him. He told me he was on his way.

I heard the key when George put it in the door. I told him I had to go home or I would get in trouble with my aunt. "Janice, they won't miss you, trust me," he said. We watched movies until we both fell asleep.

⎯ THE NEXT DAY ⎯

We were awakened by a knock on the door. It was the maid, wanting to know if we were going to stay another night or if we were checking out this morning. George told her we were leaving.

I got up and took a shower. The previous night, George had bought us his-and-hers sweat suits from Value Mart. "Where are you getting all this money you're spending?" I asked him. "I've been cutting yards and doing odd jobs for my father's friends," he answered.

After we dressed, we stopped at Jack's Burgers for breakfast. While he was ordering the food, I kept thinking how much trouble I was going to be in. My knees knocked; the more I thought about being out all night, the more afraid I became to go home. I couldn't eat. I had made myself so nervous I was sick to my stomach. George continued to tell me my aunt wouldn't notice.

"But what if she does? You don't have a place for me to live," I said. "If she does, we'll find somewhere for you to go," he said.

As we got closer to my house I asked George if he would let me off around the corner. No one would see me with him, and it would give me time to think of a lie.

Walking home, I saw Pearl outside watering her yard. She had asked me where I had been. I told her a friend's house.

"Let me take these clothes home and I'll be back," I told her. When I got to the house, the door was unlocked as usual. Some of the kids were watching television; the others were in their rooms. The only person who missed me was my little sister, and that was because she slept in the same bed. I told her I'd slept on the couch last night.

I went to the kitchen to sort out the dirty laundry. When the telephone rang, I just knew it was George. It was my aunt; my heart started beating fast.

"What are you doing?" she asked calmly. "Sorting the dirty clothes to start washing clothes," I answered.

"That's why I called," she said, "to tell you the motor went out on the washing machine while you were at work last night. I forgot to tell you this morning. Separate the dark clothes from the whites, then put them in a pillowcase, and when I come home we can go to the Laundromat." That was it. George was right. She didn't know I'd been gone all night. I could not believe it.

I washed the dishes and swept the floor. Next I reached for the mop handle in the corner next to the refrigerator, only to find it was broken. I searched through the dirty clothes for a rag to mop the floor with. I found one, tore it in half, got down on my knees, and mopped the floor. After I finished, I sat down to watch television. I thought to myself, I cannot believe I got away with staying out all night.

Robin was in her room watching television. I asked her if I could come in. She said yes. I sat on the end of her bed and asked her if she had a boyfriend. She told me he was in Texas. I asked her if she had ever thought about having sex with him. She said yes, that she'd asked her mom for birth control pills and her mom gave them to her. Robin asked me if I was thinking about having sex with the guy that killed the little girl. I told her no.

My aunt came home and I loaded the dirty clothes into the car. I told her I was ready to go to the laundromat. She started out the door, but she'd forgotten her book and turned around to get it. While she was inside the house, George drove past and honked the horn. I pretended I didn't see him.

We drove to the laundromat on Sixteenth and Roser. I took all the clothes out of the car. My aunt put the coins in to start the washers and I put the clothes in after the machine was full of water. After the clothes were in, she grabbed her book and sat down. "Aunt Gina, could you take me to get some birth control pills?" I asked. She stood up, slapped me in the face, and told me to go sit down. I went outside and called George on the pay phone, crying.

"Come get me right now. I'm on Sixteenth Street and Roser. At the laundromat!" I said. He told me he would check to see if his friend was home with the car. He would be right there, he said.

My aunt came out and told me to come inside the laundromat. I looked at her and walked away. She continued to call me, but I kept walking in the direction of the house. I walked faster, always looking back to see if I could see George coming.

I had walked about five blocks when my friend Pearl picked me up as she was driving home. I asked her if I could spend the night at her house. She told me I could.

I walked to my house and took clothes and my work uniform. I went back to Pearl's house and told her what had happened between my aunt and I. She said I could stay with her as long as my aunt didn't make any trouble.

I changed my clothes for work; Pearl dropped me off. George showed up on my job to make sure I was all right. He told me he would be back to pick me up when I got off work.

Ted waited with me to ensure that I had a ride home. I introduced Ted to George; they were already friends from grade school. Ted told George that if we ever needed the car for anything, we could just call. He gave George his telephone number and we drove off.

I took George to meet Pearl and showed him where I would be for a couple of days. George kissed me good-bye and left. I lived at Pearl's house all summer. My aunt knew where I was. She'd send messages with the kids to tell me to come home. I guessed she'd gotten tired of cleaning and washing all those clothes.

My little sister would come down to Pearl's house to see me. Often, I took her to the store to buy her clothes. I still refused to go home.

CHAPTER 7

≈ SEPTEMBER 1978 ≈

I spent all summer at Pearl's house. George and I also spent a lot of time at Big Surf, a man-made beach, and Encanto Park. On Sunday nights he was at Estaban Park, a real party place on Sundays. We had so much fun together. Everywhere he went, I was there with him. George told me that when his friends saw him without me, they would ask him where his sidekick was. I laughed when he told me.

Sex came naturally to us. The more we were together, the more we enjoyed each other. I didn't want to be on this earth without George. His voice was the first voice I heard in the morning, and the last voice I heard at night. He was my first love.

School started in a few days and I knew I wouldn't get to see much of him. He had finished high school in juvenile hall. We talked about him coming to meet me after school. The campus cops wouldn't allow him on campus during school hours.

George began doing odd jobs to save money for us to get an apartment. Occasionally he would meet me at Burger World on my lunch hour. This was my second year in high school. I tried out for junior varsity cheerleading. I needed my aunt to sign papers giving me permission to try out for the squad and take a physical, so I signed my aunt's name to the papers.

One day at practice I started feeling dizzy. I thought I'd jumped too high. It didn't last long. But that night at work I felt extremely tired. I called Pearl to ask her to come get me because I wasn't feeling well. We went to her house and I went straight to bed.

George called while I was asleep; Pearl told him I wasn't feeling good. I slept all night.

The next morning, I woke up famished. I ate, went back to sleep, and slept all day. I would get up to eat, only to fall back asleep. I thought cheerleading was wearing me out. George told me if it was taking that much out of me, maybe I should think about quitting.

Sunday morning I couldn't get out of bed; I felt weak. I had to ask Pearl's daughter Laura to help me to the bathroom. I was about to vomit, but I made it to the toilet in time. The vomit was a yellowish bitter-tasting substance. I had never felt this sick before in my life. Everything I ate came right back up.

George continued to call. I heard Pearl tell him she was going to ask my aunt for permission to take me to the hospital, and they hung up. Then Pearl called my aunt. I couldn't hear what she was saying; she'd gone into the other room to talk.

After she hung up, she walked into the den where I was lying down watching "The Price is Right." "What did she say?" I asked. "She told me she'll make you an appointment to see the doctor at the medical clinic on Monday," Pearl replied.

I got up and took a shower. Afterward, I called George to tell him I was feeling much better. I heard George tell his mom I was on the telephone and that I was feeling better.
"My mother said the weather is changing and it's probably a flu bug," George said. We talked for awhile and I told him I would meet him at the park in about an hour.

Later, walking to the park, I saw George coming toward me. But by the time I'd reached the end of the block, I heard a car horn blow as the car drove past me. It was my aunt and her husband, waving to tell me to come back to the house.

I took George's hand and we took off running. I knew my aunt and her husband had seen us, but I didn't care. I was never going back to their home. Soon George and I stopped running because I started feeling dizzy. George grabbed me to hold me up. "Girl, what is wrong with you?" he asked. "I don't know. Maybe I do have the flu," I answered. I told him to just let me catch my breath and everything would be OK.

We sat down for awhile. I looked at him, he looked at me, but the look on his face was one I had never seen before.

"Why are you looking at me like that?" I asked. He dropped his head and grabbed my hand. There was a moment of silence between us. "Let's face it, Janice, you're dying," he said seriously. I looked at him, then he busted out laughing. I hit him and told him to quit playing. He said he just wanted to make me laugh. We walked around the park, then went to play ping-pong. We stayed at the park until sunset. George walked me home to Pearl's.

WEDNESDAY MORNING

Last night my aunt called Pearl's house to tell me to be in front of South Mountain High School at 10:00 a.m. My doctor's appointment was at 10:30.

When the bell rang at the end of my second-period class I walked outside to the front of the school and watched the cars drive by, looking for my aunt. She pulled up to the curb and I got into the car. Nothing was said between us. She could tell I still had an attitude. I faced the window the entire ride to the doctor's.

When we arrived at the doctor's office my aunt filled out paperwork. Thirty minutes later, the nurse called us into the exam room. I told her the way I had been feeling and that I couldn't keep any food in my stomach. The nurse took me to the back and handed me a cup and a paper wipe, telling me to urinate in the cup.

This reminded me of the time I'd had to pee in a cup when I was a little girl. "I guess nothing bad happened. They still want me to pee in a cup," I said to myself.

"Excuse me?" the nurse responded. I told her I was just talking to myself.

I took the cup, went to the restroom and did what the nurse asked. When I came out of the restroom, the nurse told me to have a seat in a chair so she could take some blood. When she finished, I went back into the waiting room where my aunt was watching television. We waited about an hour before the doctor called us back into the exam room. He asked me how I was feeling at the moment. I told him I was tired and sleepy. He said those feelings were normal for my condition.

My aunt asked him what my condition was. He told her I was pregnant, and my aunt almost passed out. She looked more terrified than I did – and I was terrified – yet I was the one who was pregnant. The doctor told my aunt that because I was 15 and a minor, she would have to get my prescriptions filled for vitamins and iron pills.

Then it hit me. I had a baby inside of me. The doctor and my aunt went on talking. I didn't know what to feel. I froze. The doctor handed me something and walked out of the office.

We left the medical building. My aunt couldn't wait to give me a piece of her mind. She started by calling me Miss Ann (a nasty name for fast girls in my neighborhood).

"Your fast ass done got pregnant. Whose baby is it? It is that boy who killed that girl, huh?" She went on to say that I was to go to Pearl's house and get my clothes and bring them home or she would call the police. She continued, "You are going to go to a school for pregnant girls. You are an embarrassment to me, and I don't want anyone to see you pregnant. You better be glad I don't believe in abortions because you would sure have one," she finished angrily.

I didn't say anything the rest of the way home. Everything my aunt said went in one ear and out the other. I was more worried about how to tell George I was pregnant. George and I had played around and joked about having kids, but this was the real deal.

I went to Pearl's house and got my clothes. I told her I was pregnant and my Aunt Gina was so angry that she couldn't think straight. Pearl told me she knew I was pregnant and that if she could help in any way, she would.

I walked with my things to my aunt's house. She was still fussing and told the whole neighborhood I was pregnant. I asked her why she was outside telling my business. "You don't have no damn business," she answered, still mad.

"Oh, I got some," I said as I walked in the house. That made her even angrier. I knew she couldn't hit me because I was pregnant, so I said whatever I wanted to say to her.

I waited until my aunt had cooled off and gone to her room. I knew once she'd gone to her room she would be there for the night. When I called my job and told them I wouldn't be able to work that night because I wasn't feeling good, they told me they no longer needed me because I called in sick too often.

Now I have no job and a baby on the way, I thought to myself. I knew I'd never be able to move with no job. I had better call George so he'll get a job faster, I thought.

The telephone rang four times before George answered it. "I called down to Pearl's house and she told me your aunt made you come home. Why?" he asked.

"Today we went to the doctor's office and the doctor told my aunt that the reason I was sick all the time was because I'm pregnant," I told him.

"What!" he screamed before he hung up the telephone.

I tried all night to call him back, but the line was busy. I couldn't understand why he wouldn't talk to me. I thought that maybe this was his way of being in shock. I didn't know what to do. After a while I fell asleep.

The next day Aunt Gina took me out of South Mountain High to enroll me in a school called Cyesis. This was a school for pregnant girls. I was very upset that she would try to hide my pregnancy and treat me like I had a handicap.

The first day was crazy. I had to ride the bus in order to get to school. After the first day, when I got on the bus to go home, a pregnant girl named Linda told me I was sitting in her seat. She and her friends wanted me to move. Linda stood up and grabbed me by my shirt. I started hitting her in the face. The bus driver pulled over. He couldn't believe that two pregnant girls were fighting. He asked me to sit in my seat and asked Linda to sit at the front of the bus. Linda told me it was not over, and that when we got downtown, she was going to fight me again.

The bus arrived downtown. I got off the bus immediately and started walking toward the bus terminal. I heard Linda say I had better be glad her bus was at the terminal, or we'd be fighting again. She got on her bus and left.

I sat in front of the bus stop waiting for bus number one. When I happened to glance across the terminal, I saw George. My heart dropped. I walked swiftly toward him, calling his name. He turned around and saw me calling him.

When he saw me, he started walking in the opposite direction. I couldn't believe it. As close as we had been, this was how I was now being treated by him. It really hurt my feelings. I went to the front of the terminal to catch my bus. It was a long ride home.

~~~ THE NEXT DAY ~~~

On my way home from school the next day, I saw George again. This time I followed him. He looked back, saw me, and started walking faster. By the time I reached the corner, he had disappeared.

I walked back to the bus terminal to wait for my bus. As I waited, tears rolled down my face. It was so hard for me to accept the way George was treating me. I'd thought we would be together forever. I raised my head up to look across the street, hoping to see George one more time. He never came back to the bus terminal. And somewhere in the tears and tissues, I had missed my bus.

"Why are you crying?" a deep voice said. I looked up. There, standing over me, was a guy wearing a white shirt and blue jeans.

I remember staring at his Levis because they looked so stiff. He was a very dark-skinned boy my age.

"Hi," I said softly. He asked me why I was crying. I told him the whole story in about an hour. He wrote his name and telephone number on a piece of paper. "Marcus, that's a cute name," I said. He told me that if I ever felt like talking, I should call him and he would be my friend. That made me feel a lot better.

I called Marcus as soon as I made it home. We talked about everything. Marcus went to Phoenix Union High School. He told me he didn't have to take a bus from his school because it was within walking distance. We arranged to meet every day at the terminal. If I arrived there before he did, I'd wait for him; and if he made it there before I did, he would wait for me. Sometimes we wouldn't go home. We'd go to the movies, or he'd walk me around telling me how much exercise I needed to have in order to deliver a healthy baby. Marcus was a fun person to be around.

One day after Marcus's bus had pulled off, I sat waiting for mine, and three girls came up to me and asked me if I knew him. I told them that yes, he was a friend of mine.

"Well, my name is Starla, and you better stay away from my boyfriend," she demanded. I told her OK. They walked away.

The next day, as I sat in the terminal looking for Marcus, Starla appeared out of nowhere and jabbed her finger in my face. "Didn't I tell you to stay away from my boyfriend!" she yelled. Before she'd even finished yelling, I had slapped her hand away from my face. We started fighting.

Another girl named Angie pulled her away from me and told her to fight someone who wasn't having a baby. Angie walked with me to the other side of the terminal. Then Marcus came running to see if I was OK. I told him I was all right. "You could have told me you had a girlfriend," I said angrily.

"We broke up a long time ago," he said. Then I saw George walking in front of the bus terminal. I told Angie and Marcus I'd be back. I called out George's name.

He turned around. "What do you want, and why are you telling everyone that's my baby in your stomach? That is not my baby, and stop telling people that!" he yelled, and walked away.

I froze and could not believe it. My heart felt sliced into tiny pieces and smashed. "Why are you doing this to me?" I demanded as I followed him. Suddenly he stopped, walked toward me, and shoved me. I stumbled backward and my shoe came off. George picked it up and threw it in the street. "Stay away from me!" he screamed, and he walked away again.

I turned to get my shoe from the middle of the street, but Angie had picked it up, and she brought it to me. I saw Marcus across the street watching. Angie and I walked back to where he was standing. Nobody said anything. We all got on our buses and left.

THREE MONTHS LATER

My baby was due in a week, one day before Marcus's birthday and a week before mine. The official due date was March 30. The doctor said I could deliver the baby anytime from two weeks before the due date to two weeks after. I was tired of being pregnant. Sometimes the baby's foot would get into my ribs and just stay there. It was painful. I wanted to wear normal clothes like other people. I was anxious to just get it out of me. All the excitement of feeling my baby kick had worn off, and I just wanted it out of my stomach.

I sat on the couch watching television one day when my aunt's husband came into the living room and asked me to walk to the store and get him a pack of Winstons. The store was a mile away and it was 116 degrees outside.

"It's too hot out there. I'm not walking to the store," I said.

Before I even finished what I was saying, Charles popped me in the eye, leaving it swollen and red. I ran out the door and down the street to Pearl's house.

Pearl called the police. When they arrived, we walked to my aunt's. Charles denied hitting me and told the police that a lot of kids lived in this house and fought all the time. The police told him that if he hit me again, they'd take him to jail. They gave me a card to call if it happened again. I asked the officer if I could stay at Pearl's house. He told me I could only stay until my aunt got home from work.

When she did get home, Charles told her what had happened. She didn't say anything to me, but she allowed me to spend the next week at Pearl's.

⤙ **MARCH 30, 1979** ⤚

I woke up around 8:00 a.m., went to the kitchen and found a brown paper bag. I went to my room and packed my baby's clothes and diapers. At about 10:00 a.m. I went to the bus stop to take the bus to the hospital – to have my baby.

I walked into the hospital at the other end of the trip feeling such relief. I was finally going to have this baby. I'd always wondered if it was a boy or a girl. I didn't have a name in mind. I handed my paper bag to the nurse at the admission window and she took me to the delivery room.

She asked me if I was experiencing pain, but I told her no. She said that if I didn't have any pain in about 30 minutes, she would send me home. I became furious and raised my voice.

"I'm supposed to have my baby today," I said. The nurse in charge heard the commotion and instructed the first nurse to dress me in a gown and allow me to walk around. The head nurse also said that if I didn't go into labor in an hour, the other nurse was to send me home.

I walked around and looked in the window at the other babies. I saw a girl from my school who had just had her baby. Charlotte had just had a baby boy. I walked with her to her room. While we were talking, I heard something pop, and water started running down my legs. I told Charlotte that either my water had broken or I was sitting there peeing on myself.

She called a nurse, who walked me back to labor and delivery and told the delivery nurse my water had broken. When the delivery nurse saw it was me, she said skeptically, "Sure." But the head nurse told another nurse to check me. She laughed and said, "It has broken, all right."

One hour and 50 minutes later I delivered a baby girl. Her name was Erika.

A few days later my aunt picked me up and took me home from the hospital. I was glad to be able to wear normal clothes. I was out running around a week after I had the baby.

I called Angie and told her I had a little girl. Angie asked me if I wanted to play softball with a league called P.A.L. (Police Activities League). I told her yes – I'd forgotten I had this baby and I couldn't just get up and go. I took Erika everywhere I went; I had to.

At one point I wanted to go to the record hops, a popular Friday night party for teenagers. But couldn't, because I had this baby. My aunt made sure she didn't baby-sit. I couldn't work, I couldn't go places and do things the girls my age were doing because I had this baby. I became angry and resentful toward this little baby.

One day after a softball game one of the girls, who was playing with Erika, asked me if she could take Erika home. I said sure, and handed her the diaper bag.

"Janice, here's my phone number if you want to check on her," Diane said. "My mother is going to spoil her." I had never been so happy in my life.

Later that evening, Diane called and said her mother, Ellen, wanted to talk to me. She asked me if Diane had my permission to keep the baby over the weekend. I said yes. Ellen told me to feel free to call and check on the baby.

The weekend turned into months. I would visit Erika on the weekends. Ellen told me to take my time finding a job and an apartment; she would keep Erika until I was in a better position to take care of her.

I never went back to high school. I needed to find a job in order to be able to take care of my baby. In the beginning, I found a part-time job at Jack's Burgers. I lived with Pearl until my aunt brought the police to her house. I didn't want any trouble, so I left. I called Angie and she met me downtown. We talked; she asked her mother if I could live with them until I found a place of my own.

CHAPTER 8

❧ ON MY OWN ❧

After a year, I was made shift manager at Jack's Burgers. My work hours were 3:00 p.m. to midnight. This Jack's Burgers was on a street where drug dealers and prostitutes hung out. It was convenient for them because it was open 24 hours. Everything that could go on outside the restaurant did go on, from needles stuck in arms to hookers turning tricks.

The manager allowed me to hire and carry out my own ideas for my shift. I hired all my friends.

One night there was a disagreement with an order at the drive-through window. The customer asked to speak to the manager, so I went over to the window. The first thing I noticed was the car. It was a '64 Chevy Impala, pearl white with a chrome dashboard. Inside the dashboard vent were dimes.

"Wow," I said as I came to the window. The driver asked me if I wanted to go for a ride. His name was Paul, and he wrote his name and phone number on napkins and gave them to me.

I asked him what the problem with his order was. He told me, "Never mind," and said to call him. I took his number, put it in my purse, and went back to work.

⟶ THREE WEEKS LATER ⟵

I found a one-bedroom apartment. I saw a daycare center down the street from the complex and went in to see if they had room for a toddler. They did. I called Ellen, telling her I was now ready to take Erika and that I would pick her up on Saturday.

The first week of having my little girl, I was very excited, especially when I got off work to pick her up. By the second week, I was bitter. I couldn't hang out with my friends and go to the parties and parks on Sunday nights because I had this baby. I called Ellen and told her I wasn't ready. She picked Erika up before I went to work. Erika was very happy to see her. I knew then that my baby was being taken care of.

Later that day I arrived at work. All the employees were asking for the day off for a concert coming to Tempe. I wanted to go too. I was in the back office doing the scheduling when Sherrie told me someone wanted to see me. I went out to see who it was, and it was Paul, the guy with the funky six-four Chevy.

"Since you never called, I came to see if you'd go with me to the concert on Saturday," he said. I gave him my phone number.

He called after I got off work. We talked all week. I asked him if he had a girlfriend, and he said no. But he and his daughter's mother had been together for a while before they broke up.

⟶ CONCERT WEEKEND ⟵

I shopped all day to find something to wear to the concert. I finally picked out a pink outfit with a matching sweater because I knew it would get cooler after sunset.

Paul picked me up at my apartment at 5:00 p.m. The concert was to start at 6:00. Paul parked his car next to friends of his who had lowriders that hopped. The concert was nice and I saw many of my friends there.

After the concert Paul took me home. He parked the car and walked me to the door. I asked him what he would be doing the next day. He told me nothing. So I asked him if he would pick me up from a little store on the west side at about 2:00 p.m. He gave me a different number than he had previously and told me to call him when I was finished shopping. I kissed him good night and told him I'd see him tomorrow.

── THE NEXT DAY ──

The next morning I woke rather late from being out all night. I got up, washed clothes, and cleaned my apartment. By the time I'd finished, it was time to take the bus to the store.

I threw on some old blue jeans and a white T-shirt and walked down the street to catch the bus. I must have missed the first bus, because it was awhile before a bus arrived at the bus stop.

It let me off on Eleventh Avenue, where I crossed the street. I went into the store, did my shopping, and called Paul. He said he would be at the store in 10 minutes. I stood outside and waited for 20 minutes before Paul's white Impala turned the corner.

"What took you so long?" I asked.

"I had to go get gas," he answered. We were putting the food into the trunk when a blue Chevy Corvette pulled up beside us. A light-skinned lady jumped out and started putting her finger in Paul's face and cussing at him. I couldn't understand what she was saying.

Paul said, "Janice, get in the car." I got in and then Paul got in. I asked Paul who she was. "That's my daughter's mother, Marty," he said. "I'm going to take you home. Just go in the apartment and I'll talk to her." I said OK.

Marty started driving alongside Paul's car, yelling and screaming. She raised a black bag and waved it at us, saying she was going to shoot me. I asked Paul if she owned a gun. He told me she did, but that he didn't know if she had it with her.

"Thanks a lot for the mess you got me into. How do I get into my house without getting shot?" I asked him. He looked scared too.

We made it to my apartment. Paul parked the car. Before he could turn off the engine, I got out of the car and ran. I didn't want to be shot. I saw Marty get out of her car and come toward me.

I ran up the stairs to my front door, trying to quickly get the key in the door. I kept looking back at her as she came toward me, cussing all the way. It felt like it took forever to get the key in the door. As I opened it, Marty was just arm's length away.

Finally the door opened. I ran to the kitchen and picked up a knife that was on the counter. She came after me swinging and I swung my fist at her. Each time I took a swing at her, I cut her with the knife. She looked down, saw the blood racing down her arm, and ran out the door.

I picked up the phone and dialed 911.
"If you cut someone with a knife," I asked the operator, "do you go to jail?" She kept me on the phone for about 20 minutes, asking me questions.

I looked up and the police were standing outside my door. It had been left open when Marty ran out. "Are you Janice?" they asked.

I nodded. I could hear the officer on the other end of the radio, telling one of the officers that Marty was cut badly. The officer replied that he believed he had his suspect – me.

Deep inside I knew I was going to jail, because when I'd stabbed Brad as a child, the officer had told me I wasn't old enough to go to jail – but I knew I was old enough now.

The officer came up behind me and told me to stand up and put my hands behind my back. It reminded me of John's arrest, when the FBI agents took him out of the bathroom.

"She was hurt pretty bad. You better hope she lives, or you'll stay in jail for murder," the officer told me. What he said scared me. I didn't want her to die.

The ride to the police station was long and scary. The officer at the hospital with Marty continued to radio reports to the officer I was riding with, giving him the same update each time – that Marty was in critical condition. I heard my driver tell the officer at the hospital that he was going to book me on an aggravated assault charge, and that if the victim died, he'd charge me with murder.

My heart sank as I heard those words. When the officer helped me out of the car, my legs buckled. I didn't want her to die. After fingerprinting me, the officer took me to a holding cell. It had a triple bunk bed.

I stood with my head against the cell bars, hoping Marty wouldn't die. I paced back and forth between the bunk bed and the cell bars.

Then I heard an announcement on the radio. "Woman stabbed three times by Janice Higgins. The victim is in critical condition. Higgins has been booked into the county jail for aggravated assault." This was announced repeatedly over the next 12 hours. I was terrified. If they were announcing this on the radio, it must *really* be serious.

I climbed up on the top bunk, curled up in a fetal position, and began to cry hysterically, begging God not to let her die. I kept thinking, Will she die? Will I be here for murder?

The continuing life journey unfolds in…
There Were No Parents Here, Series 2, No Direction.

Acknowledgments....

$\mathcal{E}$velyn Jones
The Greatest Step-Mother in the world.
You are Heaven Sent!

$\mathcal{M}$ike Anderson & Aundria Evans
"I Love You"

$\mathcal{J}$oe & Willeen Cooley
Thank You!

$\mathcal{W}$ill and Marla Wassersug,
I appreciate all you have done for me.

*A*cknowledgments....

---

*R*ob Harrington for encouraging me
to continue to write this book.
You are truly a blessing.

A special thank you to my family and friends in recovery.
This is a journey that we have trudged together.
You will always be a part of my life.

*T*o my co-workers at St. Vincent De Paul
for helping me grow in the direction
in which I am taking my life.
Your teamwork is awesome!